Peranakan People of the Straits Settlements

Sino-Malay Ethnoculture of the Babas & Nonyas

Hugh M. Lewis

1993

ISBN

9798415883059

(Copyright © 2000, by Hugh M. Lewis)

Ethno-Cultural Studies
Indie Anthropology
Poor Hugh's E-Press
Lewis Micropublishing

The points of view expressed in this book, <u>Peranakan People of the Straits Settlements: Sino-Malay Ethnoculture of the Babas and Nonyas,</u> are those exclusively of the original author, Hugh M. Lewis, and do not represent the point of view or opinion any other person or entity in the world.

A
Bare barb
Stinging touch
Thorn among roses
Blooming in all seasons
Hearts always open to the world
Enduring, happy and sad, everlasting
Ever inviting, enticing, romancing
Your patience long lasting
Through rain and sun
Yet blossoming
Then wilting
Falling
And
Fallen
One by one
From off the hip
Petals stir in the breeze
Colorful flames float upon the water
Perfumed clouds drift between heaven and earth
Blowing with the leaves across mountains and valleys
Lost within the lengthening shadows of the twilight
Beneath the evening moon and morning stars
Ephemeral moments so enchanting
Brief spell finally broken
Simple serenity
And beauty
All gone
But
Tell me
If you can
Where are they now?
My daughters of the soil

For my two Nonyas, and my Baba
Three generations under the Ancestors' Shadows

Contents

Foreword (2022)

This is a 30-year-old republication of a set of studies on the Babas and Nonyas, particular to the Straits Settlements through the Straits of Malacca, on the West coast of the Malayan Peninsula.

These settlements originally included Penang and Province Wellesley on the mainland directly across from Penang; Singapore Island; Malacca; and the Dindings, including mainland areas on the Dinding River and Pangkor Island.

These places were the realms of the rise of the so-called "Babas and Nonyas" reputedly stretching between the late 15th Century through the early 20th Century, if not earlier. These people are also referred to more generally as the Peranakan, which would include the Totok Chinese at least of Sumatra across the Malacca Strait, and possibly on other large and smaller islands across the Indonesia archipelago, including the west, south and northern coasts of Borneo.

The Peranakan ("Babas and Nonyas" in Georgetown, Singapore and Malacca) were a creole cultural elaboration of Overseas Chinese communities that occurred in those areas dominated by Moslem majority populations and royal hierarchy that had been colonized primarily by the British, the Dutch, and previously and to a lesser extent, the Portuguese.

A lot of new research and publication has been done since these studies on various aspects of the Peranakan but many of the basic questions of the problem remain well rooted to their historiography. The Internet has proven over-all a boon to this work, as a lot of former Peranakan descendants have been able to reach out to one another now scattered around the world, and

Foreword

to easily gather knowledge resources and share previously unpublished photographs, anecdotes, and family histories.

According to the last time I researched the Babas and Nonyas on Wikipeidia.org, estimates of descendant populations range from well above four and closer to eight million souls, found in traditional homelands but now also scattered like geese abroad across the entire globe.

I present and organize this work for two purposes—to summarize older research done on the Peranakan, and to introduce people to a form of ethnocultural studies that hopefully represents a kind of wedding of the two sister disciplines, archaeology and socio-cultural anthropology.

While the archaeologists are great at digging, they may not be as good in interpreting what they dig up. While the anthropologists may be great at interpreting, at least in theory if not always in practice, they may not have been so great in excavation.

This is not to say either that all archaeologists are poor in interpretation (we have significant work in this regard, as in contextualizing frames of reference,) nor that anthropologists are necessarily poor at excavation, but the layers of culture anthropologists seek to expose are not just the same as the layers of material artifacts archaeologists like to remove from the soil.

If there is a bit of redundancy within these studies, it has primarily been for the sake of bringing to the surface emphasis on various aspects of a larger general problem set framed by the name "Peranakan" that otherwise remained buried within the literature. It is a kind of haruspication of the texts, turning it inside out to divine what may be missing on the surface.

Preface

I first wrote this manuscript I entitled <u>Peranakan</u> in 1992, based upon extensive bibliographic research and a modicum of first-hand experience in a contemporary Malaysian setting accompanying my Nonya wife (in Georgetown, Penang Island, Malaysia).

The challenge of the <u>Peranakan</u> was to demonstrate alternative ethnocultural identities that are possible when political interests and other communalistic cleavages serving to segregate and divide people in the world become contraposed. Political changes can often create long-lasting boundaries and conflicts where none may needed to have existed in the first place.

There are two wonderful and at least superficially contradictory processes that occur in the historical development of any cultural grouping of people who are trans-posed and situated trans-generationally in a plural national setting, or who become transplanted trans-nationally, in relation to other, alternative groupings with whom they may have come into contact on some limited but regular basis.

The first, natural tendency is for the development of isolating variations and differences, as demonstrated for instance in dialectical variation, that serves to partition people into ever more local and often complicated but well marked geo-historical configurations. All languages, and all cultures, tend toward this process of increasing differentiation, and it is analogous very much to the process of speciation in evolution.

Peranakan

The apparently contraposed tendency is the process of homogenization, amalgamation and accommodation that frequently accompanies related structural processes of centralization, functional integration and the superimposition of a national set of cultural standards or norms upon the daily lives of different people as a part of the complex constituency of nation-state.

In modern Malaysia the promotion of standard Bahasa Malay in government, schoolhouses and universities, as well of course in the media, serves to promote these integrative tendencies in a society that may be characterized as radically plural.

Thus we end up historically with nation-states, sometimes very large ones, like the USSR for instance, that may encompass and span a vast range of different people under a common umbrella of a central governmental administration and national identity, a common standard language, and a common ideo-religious orientation (in the CCCP's case, Marxist-Stalinism.)

It is quite obviously evident that what has made culture different from genetics is that, unlike species that allopatrically evolved into two or more reproductively isolated groupings, cultures have always offered us the historical possibility of horizontal dissemination and acculturation of individuals passing between cultures, and of two or more cultures coming together in time or place with a fusion of elements from alternative cultural orientations, sometimes even leading to production of entirely new cultural patterns.

This process may be the consequence of some colonial framework that tends to cast people from different groups into a common mixing pot for the purposes of the organization of production. Or else it may happen in a vacuum of any larger historical framework as the result of interchange and exchange between people. Of course, colonial administrative apparati can offer forces that serve to overcome the kinds of isolating mechanisms and boundaries that may have otherwise served to separate into "ethno-niches" distinct ethnocultural groupings as distinctive entities.

In this regard, anthropological ethnology within larger state contexts, may not be too unlike analogically at least biological ecology, in that we can talk about complex the differentiation and stratification of such systems across functional trophic levels of who eats what and who gets eaten.

In the modern period, the rise of new nationalisms in underdeveloped post-colonial (or neo-colonial) nation-states has often been accomplished at the expense of one or more other groups in favor of those who have gained the upper hand of power and change-controlling interests within the national society.

In such contexts, the promulgation of national integration, as in Malaysia, can proceed on a separatist basis linking ethno-nationalism to religion that serves to somewhat conveniently identify some other minority group as a marginal "out-group."

It is possible to imagine that in a more democratic and less authoritarian context, the relations between the main minorities in Malaysia might have proceeded along another set of lines than what appears to have happened, if at least the elections in such states did not so often result in ethno-political violence and race riots. (A symptom of weak authoritarian government struggling with a fledgling democratic system.)

There is a sense, on a very basic level of personality inventories and behavioral observations, that different kinds of Malaysians, whether they are Malay, Chinese or Indian, share as much in common, as Malaysians, with a shared national heritage and culture, just as they share in differences in terms of religion, social values and other basic communal cleavages.

National policies, promulgated by Mahathir under the aegis of control of his UMNO party, appear to have served two sets of competing and basically contradictory interests at the same time.

In one sense it has forged a strong national identity among most Malaysians, but in another way it has structurally embedded and perpetuated those "racial" distinctions between the different ethnocultural groupings through systematic "positive action" (affirmative action) policies that has drawn an official line between what it means to be a Malay on one hand, and what it means to be Chinese or Indian, on the other hand, versus what it is to be "Malaysian" in a multi-cultural/multi-racial sense. Thus the saying: "Malaysia for the Malays," is not the same as saying "Malaysia for the Malaysians."

To apply this example to one closer to my own homeland, I must wonder how much sixty-odd years of systematic efforts of the U.S. government in affirmative action programs and policies have shifted the social demographic landscape of our big nation. Such a program having served primarily minority interests, it may have also served equally as much or more to maintain the basic bureaucratically reified and social constructs of ideologies of race, ethno-national identities, cultural narratives, cleavages and boundaries between ethnocultural groupings, than to have broken down or eroded these kinds of boundaries in a highly stratified society.

In these reified ethno-nationalisms we can see a kind of self-fulfilling prophecy and the social construction of ethnocultural differences along racial lines in a kind of ethno-schismogenesis based more on skin color and ethnic stereotypes than upon genuine ethnocultural differences.

If we look beneath the superficial aspects of skin color, one will find that black Americans and white Americans, on average, share greater cultural affinities than they share differences, except where issues of class and history have served to demarcate and segregate these communities unevenly along racial and racist lines.

Most black Americans would find, for instance, that they share more in common with their white counterparts in the U.S., than they would share with Kenyans or Ugandans from the African Continent. White Americans undoubtedly experience the same acute sense of what it means to be an American when they mix with Europeans from the "old country."

We can look back the other way, as for instance it was quite obvious that my Malaysian Chinese wife would get along much more smoothly with Muslim Malays from her own homeland, in-spite of sometimes strongly demarcated socio-political discriminations, than she could with mainland Chinese of the PRC, even though her own ancestor's had once come from China.

At any rate, in a Malay dominated Malaysia where national elections rule in periodic cycles, that draws a strict socio-structural boundary between Chinese and Malay, in-between ethnocultural orientations as represented by the creolized Peranakan orientation, are no longer allowed to exist or possible as functionally recognized and legitimized minorities.

Peranakan

All relations between ethnocultural groupings that would permit this possibility are sundered by bureaucratically reinforced separation between the groups.

An analogy of this exists in U.S. history in the schism separating the Native Americans from the white communities that followed the trailblazers to the Old West. It is evident that upon the plains and prairies of the U.S., a full generation or two before the coming of white farmers and the U.S. cavalry to protect them, there was an extensive, full-blown "half white" Métis cultural orientation that was well developed with horse and cattle road-ranches throughout the west, decades before any farmers showed up to stake land-claims and state governments became formally recognized or organized.

This orientation was not based only upon the amalgamation between French fur traders and their squaw wives, as almost fifty percent of the fur traders were not French, but of Scottish and American descent and surname, and even of black American extraction as well.

These people had forged a unique ethno-cultural orientation on the plains that was represented by several generations of offspring who were fully involved in their Creole cultural amalgamation, including calico dresses, square dances, horse rearing and Indian trading at seasonal rendezvous and outposts.

Subsequent events associated with the appropriation of Indian lands for white settlement, gold, and the internal colonization of Indians upon remote reservation lands, led to the demise and fracturing of the basis of this in-between Métis ethnocultural orientation, which, if allowed to thrive, might have resulted in an entirely different history of relations between Native Americans and the "white" European Americans.

But of course, the rise of the Peranakan in the Straits settlements, like the rise of the North American Métis on the central plains of North America, where once only bison roamed, was part of a larger episode of history, in the former case, the British (and earlier Dutch) colonization of Malaysia, and in the latter case, the penetration of the American Old West by the great fur trade companies. When these larger structures of history passed away, so too did those groupings of people who were most closely attached to these frameworks. But the descendants in both cases stuck around and remember from their grandmother's stories a different kind of world.

In publishing these texts, I have sought to present the "Peranakan problem" as one that is intrinsically interesting from a theoretical and anthropological point of view, not only because of the unusual processes of amalgamation that are so important to these patterns, but also for the case of exemplifying basic and distinctive ethnocultural models.

From this standpoint, these studies fit clearly within an ethnocultural methodology that attempts to relate the life-experiences and daily events and attitudes of culture bearers to the larger historical and cultural contexts that unfold more gradually and imperceptibly in the background of their lives.

I first attempted this approach in studying and seeking to understand the predicament of Vietnamese "boat people" who had eventually found themselves washed up on the shores of a distant and very different new homeland that was not traditionally their own.

Relating the large, regional and general frames of reference to the immediate, concrete, little everyday events, and trying to make sense of the systemic relationships and patterns involved in the articulation of the lives of these people, invoked an additional requirement of attempting to understand in a comprehensive manner the knowledge, or the social construction of information, the traditions and cultural heritage relating to these people, mostly by "cultural studies at a distance."

Thus, doing ethnocultural fieldwork was more than merely doing ethnographic fieldwork, which usually involved hanging out with people for extended periods of time while trying to take legible notes. It became like ethno-history, the full detailed hermeneutic and philological excoriation of all evidence, textual and otherwise, surrounding and relating to and serving to demarcate the identity of a group of people as somehow a distinctive culture.

Subsequent to the first work with the Vietnamese refugees, that culminated successfully I believe in a fairly well integrated ethnocultural approach, I have had and made for myself the opportunity to conduct similar research with the Hokkien Chinese of Malaysia, with Modern Malaysians, the Peranakan, and later, the Métis of North America.

Each study presented unique challenges to the technical and formal problem of the ethnocultural study of people. Each presented new forms of understanding about ethnocultural studies in both a larger and more general sense and in terms of detailed operational approaches.

This work was a significant part of that effort. It is presented here in two sets, an earlier version which was done in requirement for an Ethno-history seminar that I had taken with Dr. Ray Wood, and the second version (entitled Nonya) that was rewritten to fulfill requirements for another technical writing seminar I had undertaken with the same professor the following year.

I present the first work in these pages, followed by the second version in a follow-on text, entitled "The Overseas

Chinese: Ethnocultural Studies of the Nanyang Chinese," because web-publishing makes it easy to do so, as well as to demonstrate the progression of the development of ideas relating to ethnocultural studies that are associated with this research upon the Peranakan peoples in relation to other people and ethno-cultures in the world.

The order and presentation of this work in the mid 1980s to mid-1990s, was originally intended to reflect the methodological organization and operationalization of formal ethnocultural studies as a distinctive and well-defined form of anthropological inquiry that is both theoretically interesting and methodologically rewarding.

A word of note concerning the term "ethnoculture" (variously spelled as "ethno-culture.") I have found it used rarely if at all in the literature, but my encounter with the concept goes back to my work with Vietnamese American refugees in the early 1980s, many of whom were de-facto ethnic Chinese, which work brought me into touch and awareness of much of the literature upon the Nanyang Chinese, especially the significant and timely works of Judith Strauch. The concept of "ethnoculture" I found enunciated in terms most closely associated with "ethnic mosaics" in the work of Judith Nagata, and I credited therefore, perhaps naively, the concept of ethno-culture to be more of a Canadian than an American academic concept.

It is important to emphasize that ethnoculture is not isomorphic with or the same as or part of ethnic studies per se as these have become elaborated in many different departments, or even growing into their own departments, over the last five or six decades marked by the celebration of human diversities and the second-guessing of our own ethnocentrisms (if not always associated egocentrism.)

Peranakan

As such, ethno-culture in the lower case was never a substitute anthropologically for "Culture" in the upper case, as suggested by one of my dissertation advisors at my defense. Ethno-culture relates most closely to ethno-history as I've been somewhat engaged in this work as well, closely aligning with proto-historical and historical archaeology.

But going back to my earlier Master's Thesis work, represented in this set of texts in the title "<u>Boat People: Ethno-Culture of the Vietnamese Refugees</u> {1984-1986)" as well as by planned subsequent works, ethno-culture is its own methodological approach stressing comprehensiveness of literary and textual research, combined with multi-disciplinary efforts at contextualization of understanding of people's places and movements in the world, integrating the individual culture-bearer within the larger social and culture historical nexus from which they came and within which they participate, change and develop during the courses of their lives.

In this sense ethnoculture is a clear methodological and research design descendant of the methods of Culture at a Distances studies devised by Margaret Mead and Ruth Benedict to productively utilize a wide array of cultural resources for analysis and synthetic description.

The study of ethno-culture would be, as Jacquetta Hawkes might want to have said, something more than just the Americanist study of a reified "culture" across space or largely through a sense of static time. Hence ethnocultural space is as much subjective as it is geographic, and ethnocultural time is more dynamically marked by developmental change and chaos than by anything neatly chronological on a clear linear timeline, or even cyclical, periodic or predictable as the spokes of the hermeneutic wheel of culture "*geisteswissenschaftliche methoden.*"

I hope in the future that I will have further opportunities to conduct similar ethnocultural studies upon other interesting groups of people in the world, and to thereby further refine and develop the systematic study of ethnoculture as hopefully a valuable contribution to world scholarship.

An updating of these works is in order by subsequent works undertaken by European scholars and by Malaysian Chinese scholars, namely Felix Chia, Ho Ming Wing and Tan Che Beng, now head of the Anthropology program at Hong Kong National University. Peranakan studies is now fairly well defined in outline, when in 1994 it remained largely disparate, largely localized, and only very vague in outline form.

These recent developments speak of the remarkable progress and growth of knowledge, both as an industry in itself, and as a function of advancing scholarship and publishing in the larger world. I am glad that Peranakan studies have come of age now in the appropriate academic departments around the world as a legitimate area of inquiry, just as I've been glad to watch my Nonya wife reconnect with her roots via social media vis-à-vis other Peranakan around the world.

Introduction: The "Peranakan Problem"

"The Baba, a product of an accident of history, is a time-traveler; he has come and he must go." (Felix Chia, <u>The Baba</u> 1980:193)

"Peranakan" is a Malay term designating a particular Creole culture of partly assimilated Chinese in Malaysia and Indonesia. To an unknown extent, these people's distinctive identities were the by-products of political-economic and culture historical forces of social integration within a colonial Southeast Asian context that arrested pre-colonial "mosaic" processes of amalgamation and assimilation, and tended to foster social isolation and structural separateness between the main groups—Europeans, ethnic Overseas Chinese, and Indigenous peoples.

With modernization dating from the turn of the twentieth century, and with the subsequent advent of new nationalisms in Southeast Asia, this sense of difference has resulted in systematic segregation, discrimination, cultural erosion and eventual disintegration of Peranakan and their cultural life-ways, who have been forced to redefine their identities in relation to dominant reference groups in more adaptive ways.

In certain places during the colonial era, especially in the so-called Straits Settlements of Penang, Malacca and Singapore, the "Peranakan" emerged as a distinctive, fully crystallized ethno-cultural orientation with its own sense of cultural focus and elaboration of distinctive, ethnically defined traits. This became the highly stylistic culture of the "Babas and Nonyas."

This culture is remarkable from an anthropological standpoint because it is predominantly "Nonya" in focal orientation—featuring the elaboration of basic traits, dress, housing patterns, residence, kinship, marriage, arts, religion, beliefs and values, entertainment and cooking, which were the principle prerogative of nearly completely domesticated womenfolk.

The men, the "Babas," active in outside, worldly affairs, were left relatively unconstrained to define their identities vis-à-vis dominant and traditional reference groups, i.e., European colonial culture and traditional and modern Overseas Chinese religious and business cultures. On the wane, we are left to ethno-historically account for this somewhat unusual cultural development, especially when we consider that it emerged from a basic Chinese cultural orientation that has always been strongly patriarchal and patrilineal in tradition.

This is only part of a more complex paradox in trying to account for the origins, influences, factors, and dimensions of an "in-between" ethnocultural grouping, whose fundamental identity has remained somewhat ambiguous in outline, and especially when we must account for its identity in "ethnic" terms which comprised seemed to comprise the basic organizational "ethos" of the people.

The entire problem is complicated by the relative paucity of substantial information about this group—the majority of ethnographic and historiographical studies of this group have been done only since World War II, within a context of modern Nationalisms—well after the time of its heyday in the Nineteenth Century and well into the post World War II period of its social disintegration.

The "Peranakan Problem" is defined in the course of this work as a number of different dimensions and themes that intersect to create certain central foci—different arguments are elucidated, not so much for the sake of creating a consensus, as for revealing contradiction.

The "Peranakan Problem" exists at several different levels of theoretical generality and methodological analysis, and is not one primary issue or hypothesis. It is as much a "problem" of the researcher's definition and terms of description and explanation as it is anything that is, or was, ever "out there" in the human world.

Like the human reality it is held to represent, it is many different things, with many different possibilities. And yet, all the theoretical and hypothetical diatribe notwithstanding, the "Peranakan Problem" can perhaps best be exemplified in the statements of a single person who is Peranakan by birth and cultural heritage.

What does the understanding of Peranakan ethnoculture and ethno-history have to contribute to general theoretical interests in cultural anthropology? What does general anthropology have to contribute to the understanding of the Babas?

Such questions serve as a fulcrum point for the movement and articulation of basic research in the world—it is a question maybe meant to be asked, but perhaps never finally answered.

The Babas represent something unusual and therefore interesting in the world, but not something that was unexpected, given the social conditions and historical contexts in which they emerged to define themselves as distinct and separate from all other people.

They are not to be facilely dismissed as but one more of many dialectical sub-groupings of the Chinese nation, but another minor variant upon a dominant theme of Sinicization, because they stand clearly apart from all other Chinese in Southeast Asia—their cultural orientation ran somewhat across the Chinese grain.

They represent a dynamic aspect of Chinese cultural character which would be considered uncommon in terms of the patriarchal and xenophobic Sinitic stereotypes—a synthetic and syncretistic capacity of Chinese to readily incorporate and assimilate foreign elements in a creative way when given the context and opportunity, and incentive, to do so, and to redefine their own identity in a way which does not always fall beneath the umbra of their very long reaching Ancestor's Shadow.

But the Babas also stand for something else that is perhaps more interesting from an anthropological standpoint—the study of their provenance in time and place, their emergence, historical elaboration, and subsequent submergence beneath the tides of modern historical developments, allow us to ask critical questions about some of foundational concepts concerning culture, ethnicity, social structure, historical patterning, and even evolutionary processes of change.

They represented an interstitial, as opposed to marginal, sub-grouping of a wider stream of humanity. Their life-ways straddled the entire rural-urban continuum, and was as much a product of the cityscape as it was of the countryside.

They were not a "band," or "tribe," or peasant village—they were not a ghetto, an ethnic enclave, a colony, a cult or sect, a caste, a class, a party or a corporate institution, and still, as an enduring yet ephemeral historical phenomenon, they were as real and distinctive as any human grouping on earth.

Peranakan

Uncommon as they have been, they did not stand completely alone in the annals of history—there have been other similar kinds of groups in other parts of the world.

To claim that the Baba Chinese were a residuum of a colonial era is only a biased part of the whole picture—the emergence of their kind is to be expected any time there has been prolonged, organized, and creative contact between different cultures, different civilizations, different "races", and different streams of history—such groups form like swirling eddies in the confluence of great rivers.

They are not so much "transitional cultures" as they are "cultures of transition"—new and emergent possibilities of cultural patterning created as a result of acculturative interchange and historical transition. They are "cultures of convergence" that are only possible when different groups of people are forced to live together in some degree of mutual symbiosis and tolerance.

From the standpoint of the study of cultural transmission and change, the case of the Babas represents an interesting model of an evolutionary process of cultural "speciation" that occurs as the consequence of acculturation.

It is the fundamental reconfiguration of basic cultural patterns as the direct result of such processes of acculturation, and the emergence of a new and viable cultural orientation with its own distinctive sense of cultural value and historical tradition.

This process of cultural convergence and speciation affects virtually every aspect of the cultural configuration—evidence for the basic changes are to be found in language, religion, arts, social structure, values, world view, dietary patterns, ethnic identity, etc.

The patterns produced by the convergence of two or more separate cultural configurations form something of a moiré that contains elements of both configurations but in a new arrangement.

With the Babas, we get a glimpse of "culture history in the making"—if not actually on the level of individual actors and their decision-making, then on the next higher level of primary social groups and communities acting in concert and in a directed manner to fashion a common sense of community with a shared history.

We can also see, in the momentous and inevitable turn of the wheels of history, the larger historical structures that remain always in the background, like the hour hand of a clock, slow and imperceptible in its movement, yet inexorable in its constraint and imperative for human action.

We can clearly see how new cultural possibilities can be created, and then taken away, by larger mitigating historical structures—if the conditions are not appropriate for the germination of culture, as for the germination of seedlings in the earth after a long and severe winter, then no amount of growth can be expected.

With the example of the Babas, the general framework of culture history can be articulated with the narrower focus upon the ethno-histories of particular peoples of particular periods and places.

With the Babas, we can get a partial picture of how cultural dynamics intermesh with historical process. We can write, and rewrite, the story of the Baba's in such a way that combines the narrative frame of historical explanation with the descriptive frame of ethnographic exemplification.

Peranakan

"Ethnos" is the study or knowledge of the life-ways of a group of people—it comes from the Greek meaning "Nation," "race" or "people."

From it are derived many of the terms central to anthropological method and theory—ethnography, ethnology, ethno-history, ethnocentrism, ethnogeny, ethnicity, ethno-nation, ethno-linguistics, ethno-musicology, ethno-science, ethno-semantics, ethno-medicine, and ethno-botany.

The central conceptual importance of "ethnos" to the field of anthropology should go without saying, and yet its centrality and significance has been left largely taken for granted—as something adjectival and dependent upon some other conceptual preoccupation.

Ethnos names a basic operative principle in the definition of human identity and difference in a social world—human history has largely been a narrative of the formation, conflict and resolution of human identities and cultural differences between different groups of people across time and space.

Ethnos also marks off a central principle in the study of the human condition in the world, of its many variations, its "grand arc" of possibility, and its basic structures of pan-humanness. Basic human identity is constituted socially and historically in the world—it is "constructed"—and then, in turn, becomes the central organizing principle for the construction of the world. We make the world in terms of how we see ourselves in it in relation to other people, and we make our own identity in terms of how we see the world of others and ourselves.

"Ethnoculture" is my designation for the distinctive identity and difference of a people that is defined both socially in relation to other groupings, and historically in terms of its origin, development and direction, in <u>terms that are emically salient for the people who are so defined.</u>

The objective of the study of ethnoculture is to discover and derive the basic principle of ethnos, as it is culturally and historically elaborated and operative in the world, as well as the factors that constrain and influence its development.

Ethnoculture is the notion of the distinctive symbolic identity that is shared and elaborated by a particular cultural grouping. It shares with ethno-history a common ground in the idea of the baseline as the point of departure and final reference in our constructions of the symbolisms and group identities of a people. For the student of ethno-history the concept of the baseline is rooted in the "ideal past" as a fossilized origin point and source for cultural development and civilization.

For the student of ethnoculture the baseline becomes translated as the "eternal present" that focuses upon the core continuities that remain traditionally conservative and fundamentally definitive of a group's worldview and distinctive identity, at least for a distinct period or a group's lifespan.

Ethnoculture inevitably involves the inseparable problems of the construction and "re-presentation" of reality, and the construction of "reconstructions" as well as the problem of defining the subjective/objective basis of group integration and the influences of change.

Thus, both ethnoculture and ethno-history centrally deal with the dilemmas of "historicity" and "facticity" in seeking primary sources and questioning the political and ideological foundations of knowledge and the tautological conundrums of theories, and hence both are needed antidotes to fast and non-reflective explanations about human experience.

Peranakan

The ethnoculture of the Babas is exemplary, and problematic, for a number of important anthropological reasons. In seeking to establish a "base-line" for "traditional" Baba Chinese culture, it will be discovered that such a "base-line" is at best only a model, a benchmark of a scattered history, an ethno-historical construction, which we need elaborate only in order to subsequently amend or refute by the discovery of contrary, alternative or supportive evidence.

The ethnocultural continuum of the Peranakan Chinese of Malaysia, Singapore, and Indonesia manifests several significant dimensions that can be referred to as social structure and process, language, religion and ethnicity.

Though the most visible Babas and Nonyas were the upper class merchants of the port cities of the Straits, and were thus very much fixtures of the urban city-scape, we can probably correctly claim that the "average" Peranakan was a petty merchant trader who was "in the middle" in a variety of senses, and also we cannot ignore a substantial number of rural Peranakan who were agricultural pioneers and entrepreneurs, or who were long settled in small village colonies that dotted the countryside.

We must therefore take into account a fairly broad range of social stratification and occupational differentiation within Peranakan communities—to be Peranakan was not to be only one kind of person, and Peranakan cultural orientation did not imply simply one set of acquired traits—it consisted more of local and regional variations upon a common theme, and even thematic variation upon a common, polythetic set of cultural features.

Peranakan social realities varied widely over both period and place—what it may have been in pre-contact Malacca, versus what it apparently had been in Nineteenth Century Singapore, to what it was to become in Indonesia or Penang in the modern, post-colonial era, may well be quite different sorts of things only somewhat spuriously subsumed under the same basic epithet.

Of course, from an ethnocultural point of view, we must assume at least one basic chain of continuity between the distant past and the immediate present and that is the linkage of cultural, if not biological, heredity—of people who are the direct descendants, whatever the number of generations removed or diluted, from those who first were known as or eventually came to be called "Peranakan," and who have subsequently since retained some minimal sense of what it is to be a Peranakan.

And in this sense of familial inheritance, early childhood socializations, primary social networks and corporate institutions, and important life experiences which become played out in the relative presence or absence of the most significant others, critically influence and shape the nature and culture of this kind of ethnocultural identity.

And in this regard, both ethnos and culture become very real and very significant social and historical forces to be reckoned with, as both come to have a molding influence upon the subjectively felt, lived experiences of the individual "culture bearer."

Both come to have a massive, basic shaping and constraining effect upon experience and interaction in the world, as both subjectively internalized and externally objectified, and as both a realizing agency of potentiality and a mediating mechanism in dealing with change, conflict and difference.

This speaks for a much deeper and more basically rooted connection between ethnos and culture than many scholars of ethnicity, who stress the communicative, social, economic and political aspects of ethnicity, seem less willing to acknowledge.

A primordialist view of the relation between ethnos and culture holds that such an identity is more foundational and less easily alterable than other kinds of identities—national, religious, social—and that these other identities might achieve some sense of ingrained embedding by their primordial connections with a people's shared ethnoculture.

There are two theoretical implications of this primordialist view of ethnoculture.

First, the basic ethnocultural continuities—the common core of a shared identity—cannot be simply negotiated away, transacted, traded in or changed "for a new suit of clothes." Though boundaries between groups are negotiated, these boundaries are always fuzzy and always encompass a more conservative "prototypical" core.

Second, the outward aspects of ethnoculture are largely historically determined, and thus the actual significances of ethnocultural identity are quite variable across space and time—the combination of the core traits are likely to be lost or added, variably mixed and interchanged.

A third implication forthcoming from the first two is that ethnocultural identity tends always to draw from the past, from its traditions, its styles, customs, habits, lessons and myths, for purposes of the present, and to appropriate elements and aspects of the present for the sake of reconstructing and overcoming the "lost sense" of the past.

This makes ethnoculture both very functionally adaptive and very conservative. This always creates a dialectical tension about ethnocultural identity that is never without some contradiction and some interesting conflicts.

Another significant dimension of the problem of Peranakan "Ethnoculture" are the social distances, contradictions and obstacles, spanned between traditional or Overseas Chinese cultural foci, on the one hand, and becoming a part of the Malay cultural tradition, on the other.

Peranakan culture was not just intermediate in the socio-structural sense of being comprised of "pariah" merchant middlemen, but they also were an in-between socio-cultural phenomena as a "transitional culture" or a "culture of transition" arrested somewhere along the process of assimilation of a minority Chinese group into the social ethos of the dominant Malay host culture.

On top of being such a culture defined somewhere along a continuum of assimilation, the Peranakan also came to constitute a "culture of amalgamation" that was defined by some modicum of ethnic intermarriage and intercultural integration. Even more problematic, we must also take into account its orientation as a "culture of acculturation", subject as it was to strong foreign influences.

And, to top all this sociological jargon off, we may speak of Peranakan as being commonly also a "culture of accommodation" in that its basis was formed in a context that promoted mutual interaction, basic reciprocities, and mutual adjustments to social differences during different historical periods. So we must again ask ourselves, what, and where, is Peranakan ethnoculture?

In this regard it is commonly assumed that the principle barrier to full assimilation of the Peranakan Chinese into the dominant Malay or Indonesian societies has been the Islamic faith that prohibited intermarriage without conversion—but evidence supports the contention that Islam was not everywhere equally the same kind of fundamental barrier to intermarriage that it has more recently and commonly become. It is also commonly contended that Malay culture and ethnic identity has been founded centrally upon the principle of being a good "fundamentalist" Muslim.

This is a legal prejudice that has become predominant in modern nation-states that failed to effectively separate church and state—but being Malay has long been something more, or else, than only being Moslem.

Conversely, it is often argued that traditional Chinese cultural identity has been founded upon the principle of ethnos that is relatively independent of any religious components. Traditional Chinese religious orientation is held to reflect the openness and syncretistic character of the Chinese social world, and the synthesizing qualities of the Chinese mind.

But evidence also suggests that there is something fundamental to the core of "Chineseness" which has basic religious overtones. The Chinese world and worldview may not always be as open as it is represented to be by much of the literature, and that Islam may not provide the only barrier to the assimilation of the "Peranakan" into the host society.

"Chinese Religionists" frequently seem to present as great a barrier to passing between Chinese and Malay worlds as anything Islam has been purported to do.

Regarding intermarriage, it is evident that interethnic social integration and cultural amalgamation can effectively proceed without the requirements of members of contraposed groups being wed, and that intermarriage is also a sociocultural possibility whether or not other processes of social integration and assimilation are occurring.

What it seems to require most is the tolerance and willing acceptance of the different families, and communities, that are thus united—and nothing can so divide brothers and families against one another as relatively remote, and frequently self-serving, political interests.

It is worthwhile to briefly speculate on the "ethno-genesis" of Peranakan ethno-culture, especially the focal and elaborate kind of "Baba and Nonya" culture that apparently developed during the Nineteenth Century in the Straits Settlements.

A romantic model would be a story of the original "Nonya" who set the entire Nonya culture snow-balling in its development through the many successive generations, from mother to daughter in an unending chain.

Was she a Chinese woman, the daughter of an Imperial emperor of China, sent to Malacca to take the hand the Malay Sultan, adopting Malay dress, Malay speech, Malay beliefs, but remaining basically Chinese to the core?

Or was she but a young outcast of a Malay Kampong, a debt-slave or a concubine of a rich Chinese Kapitan, basically Malay in most aspects but constrained in fundamental ways by a patriarchal Chinese tradition? Are the Nonyas basically Chinese or Malay?

It is not too far-fetched to imagine a relatively small group of original Nonyas of Malacca, sometime in the Sixteenth Century, who found themselves in a unique situation to create a whole new cultural pattern and civilized style, and to subsequently elaborate and hand this culture down through their daughters, essentially unchanged, until the Twentieth Century.

In this regard, it would do well to remember the subservient role of the woman in traditional Chinese society. Only as a mother and matriarch of a domestic household does a woman hope to have any power or influence, and only as this power could be realized through a father, a husband or a son, or alternatively, only through a separate status network-hierarchy of other women, mothers and daughters.

The suffocating love of the mother for the son is a fundamental cultural psychological theme of Chinese tradition and ethos. In an almost exclusively male community—male dominated in every way.

In the early trading outposts of the Nanyang, an empty niche would have been created in a displaced and makeshift Chinese cosmos—a niche that would have had symbolic, social, structural and psychological components, by the dearth of Chinese women and "mothers" that could not be simply filled by the services of a few prostitutes.

This niche would not have been an unattractive one to fill, as it had the promise of some wealth and advantage among tradition bound people who would not have otherwise realized such things. This empty niche left an opening in the traditional Chinese cosmos for the incorporation of foreign elements.

We must seriously ask why it was almost exclusively domestic and female Malay elements that came to so strongly define what was distinctive about Nonya culture, and we are left with a kind of proposition that there may be basic dimensions to its culture that were defined along lines of female and male identity respectively.

A useful kind of distinction to make is between ethno-political symbols that are primarily concerned with external boundary maintenance and ethno-religious symbolisms that involve domestic relations and conceptions of sacredness, and the association with these kinds of symbols to male and masculine domains and features, or feminine and female traits, respectively.

In the case of the Babas and Nonyas, what fell away from the tradition-bound Chinese Confucian orientation was the whole female side of its cultural orientation, to become infused, ethno-culturally, if not quite racially, with many Malay elements.

The second alternative was that Baba fathers and sons were left to fill in and play the part of "reality culture" bearers—to use Alfred Kroeber's distinction—in networks that were externally oriented to culture brokerage and the mediation of differences.

Nonya mothers and daughters were left separately to play a role in the construction and elaboration of an almost exclusive "value culture" which was almost entirely a feminine prerogative. Within domesticated social spheres, women were left to claim and compete with one another for status.

When we consider the religious orientation of the Babas and the Nonyas, we are faced with another paradox—though incorporating many Malay elements involving trance, superstition, animistic spirituality, spirit possession and ritual, the Peranakan pantheon of deities remains basically Chinese in character.

We must confront the possibility that no religion or religious system, as it is lived by an ethno-cultural grouping of people, is a purely unitary phenomenon. We only have to look to the incorporation of local deities, beliefs and cults, all over the world, into the sainthood of a strictly monotheistic Catholic orthodoxy, to see a similar kind of "lived" religion in action.

The alleged Matrilocality of the Babas and Nonyas, as a persistent and pervasive social institution, also demands some sort of explanation in terms of origins and primary causes. Bringing a young son-in-law into the household provided a handle of control of labor and other resources.

Though theirs was not a culture characterized by chronic warfare which demanded the long-term absence of the males, they were a settlement of "sojourner-traders" in which the economic interests of the males demanded long periods of absence, and they were also a group that may have always been defined by some kind of interethnic stress or tension, if not always outright conflict and competition.

It is also apparent that though the traditional Nonyas may have held the keys to the home, even the shop, as well as to whatever domestic wealth possessed by the family, they were not themselves involved in any forms of primary production or external economic activity.

Unlike many other Southeast Asian women, they were not themselves petty traders or producers. Thus we are left to explain an apparent exception to the cross-cultural rule of Matrilocality, in terms of origins and causal factors that stress the "rarity-value" of women who were in every respect a minority.

This situation may have been based upon the Nonya's reproductive role as the principle provider and care-taker of children who were brought up to think of themselves and call themselves Chinese even though they often acted and talked like Malays, and in terms of the elaboration of a strictly domestic, female-centered culture which was transmitted by processes of both primary and secondary socialization through the daughters.

The daughters became the principle culture-bearers, and inheritors of values, attitudes, and other marked characteristics that were distinctively Nonya. And if the mothers were the principle arrangers in their children's marriages, then they must have taken much care in finding suitable partners who would contribute to, rather than take from, their domestically oriented, female-focused culture.

Another paradox is that though in relation to their male relatives in a patrilineal Chinese world, the Nonya women were always in a subordinate position, at least within the interior world of their domestic households, differences of age came to override those differences based upon gender. Within their own internal world, the Nonyas came to control resources, hence power, prestige and privilege that sometimes matched or predicated that of the male Babas in the outside world.

It is even more of a paradox when we consider that young Nonya daughters still had inferior value compared to that of Baba sons—though they were the principle agents and carriers in the transmission of Nonya life-ways, they did not gain ascendant status except through marriage, motherhood and the subsequent marriage of their own sons and daughters.

The Baba boys were clearly privileged, even though from a strictly cultural point of view they would always remain peripheral, because they still were under the penumbra of the Ancestor's shadow—it was still the Confucian thing to do.

Peranakan ethnoculture, especially the distinctive form that came to bloom in the Straits Settlements during the Nineteenth and early Twentieth Centuries, was clearly something more than just a by-product of colonial political economy within a plural society.

In fact, its occurrence may have been quite separate and independent of the colonial setting, and some evidence at least suggests that the colonial framework may have actually hindered and limited its development and florescence in fundamental ways.

European colonialism did clearly serve to highlight it, to underscore its ethnocultural distinctiveness and difference in ways that it may not have otherwise been emphasized. The fortunes of the Babas and Nonyas within a foreign administrative structure were only indirect results of this contact and acculturation—the effect rather than the cause of such contact and acculturation.

It was the very between-ness of Straits Chinese society that permitted them the latitude to serve the critical role of "culture brokers" and as articulatory intermediaries within a colonial social system, a role which was effectively not available to the members of other, more tradition-bound groups.

And with their increasing wealth and structurally defined privilege and opportunity within the colonial framework, their visibility, distinctiveness, status and prestige also increased.

If the Babas and Nonyas were not directly the by-product of a somewhat superficial colonial arrangement, then they must be understood in another set of terms.

If they weren't primarily "colonial," then they were preeminently "traditional"—and what has been pulling them apart today have been larger forces of modernization that have been wearing away the fabric of many different people's cultural traditions.

What is "tradition" from a modern, secular point of view?

Values and orientations of family, lineage, respect for and preservation of the authority and legitimacy of tradition; a significant sense of the past, and a central place in one's world for religion; the primacy of the family as the principle agent of socialization and cultural transmission; values of nurturance and interdependency rather than independence and personal dominance.

"Tradition" defined the principle domain of ethno-culture.

The very factors that fostered their structural fortune in the colonial era, led to their structural misfortune, their social disintegration, their loss of visibility and status in the post-colonial era that now has to define itself along new lines, imported from the West, in terms of modernization, materialism, functional development and nationalism.

As the Overseas Chinese have come to face increasing ethnic segregation and discrimination in most modern Southeast Asian nation-states, the splitting apart of splintered ethnic segments of society and the widening gulf between indigenous majorities and Chinese minorities, has tended to pull apart and disintegrate the Peranakan who were structurally in-between two worlds layered upon one the other.

Each new generation of Baba and Nonya is left with fewer alternatives other than to attempt passing into one or another of the segments of modern society—less and less of their own culture and their own people are leftover by which to continue to construct and maintain a separate, distinctive Peranakan identity.

Because passing downhill and out of a context defined by overpopulation and fierce social circumscription and competition for very limited resources, is much easier than passing uphill against a strong current of social competition, most Peranakan have been undergoing resinification.

For some reason, becoming a Moslem in order to pass into Malay society has never been a viable option open to most

Peranakan—the losses in social status and individual identity in both Chinese and Muslim worlds would have been much greater than the few gains in social security and acceptability.

Though the Malays are in a structurally predominant and superior position to the Overseas Chinese, their place is by no means an enviable one.

Few Chinese would undergo circumcision in order to trade places with their Malay counterparts, neither in politics nor especially not in business.

The only other alternative seems to be one of escape from the Southeast Asian setting—to Singapore, or better yet, to the Commonwealth countries or to the United States. English language, Western education, the acquisition of money, material wealth, and Christianity are all efficacious vehicles for such escape.

With the disintegration of Peranakan ethnoculture, we are witnessing a kind of socio-cultural atomization of Peranakan people and communities into smaller and smaller groupings—ultimately to become enclosed as separate family units, or even as lone individuals culturally astray in the wider social stream.

With less and less social basis available for interaction in the wider world in purely Peranakan fashion, more and more Peranakan are feeling them selves cut off from their roots, from the tradition in which they themselves were raised, adrift upon the tides of change.

I: The Overseas Chinese

The Peranakan problem cannot be finally resolved if it is not sufficiently situated within a larger setting—ultimately within the framework of traditional and colonial Southeast Asian civilization.

Peranakan communities were natural outgrowths of plural worlds in which Overseas Chinese operated and within which they acculturated, assimilated, amalgamated and articulated their distinctive adaptations.

To the extent that Nanyang Chinese became merchant-middlemen or pioneering farmers penetrating the jungle hinterlands, articulating local and regional economies for indigenous peoples throughout Southeast Asia and even beyond, to the same extent the Peranakan largely emerged as mediators between Chinese communities, as well as with local indigenous societies and representatives of distant European societies within colonial contexts.

Many of the basic structural features that underlie the formation and ordering of the Peranakan world are features basic to the patterning and developmental processes of much of the Southeast Asian world—the maritime openness and outward-looking orientation; the natural, tropical environment; the role of rivers in the integration and incorporation of diverse and different ecologies within a single "interregional system;" the recurrent structural theme of the "organization of diversity;" that like the supernatural percussive melody of gamelan, reverberates in every ritual, in every myth, in every language.

Peranakan

Foremost of the themes which have united Southeast Asia as a region and which help to contextualize the "Peranakan problem" is the influence which diverse, foreign cultures have had in the stylistic and structural development of what can be referred to as a typically "Southeast Asian civilization."

Acculturation—religious, political, economic, social—has long been a perennial influence in the region, and different culture historical phases of acculturation can be used, almost in the manner of archaeological stratigraphy or stylistic seriation, to uncover the many layers of culture that have become embedded one on top of the other throughout Southeast Asia.

Each phase contributed to the development of Southeast Asia upon a new level of socio-cultural integration and structural articulation. The incorporation of foreign elements, ideas, things, and people, served as a common catalyst, a common stimulus, to the endogenous elaboration and development of Southeast Asian civilization.

Inextricably entangled with the problem of such acculturation and the incorporation of diversity, is the problem of "ethnos" as a central organizational principle of Southeast Asian civilization.

Ethnicity as the study of ethnic identity and ethno-genesis as the study of ethnic origins, are intrinsic and basic dimensions of Southeast Asian studies in general. "...Ethnic diversity is so fundamental in Southeast Asia that it is one of the great laboratories for the study of ethnicity." (D. E. Brown, 1976: 99) But this ethnicity takes shape only in modern nation-state societies, vis-à-vis public forums of resource competition.

It was in general reference to Southeast Asia, and in specific relation to the pervasiveness of the Overseas Chinese there, that had led J. S. Furnival to formulate his now classic theory of "radical pluralism"—the social integration of people of many cultures in a common market place and under the aegis of a common political structure.

Because the Peranakan were basically Chinese, members of the so-called Nanyang, the centrality of the principle of ethnos is especially important in their study, such that we may refer to a basic Chinese cultural "ethos of ethnos" that was part of the openness, organizational refinement and intricacy, and adaptability of the Overseas Chinese social system.

This brings out the central dilemma of the study of ethno-culture—the problem of determining the appropriate criteria for drawing the line between what constitutes an ethnic group, or an ethnic phenomena, or an ethnic category or identity, and what is constitutive of genuinely cultural ethos and difference, cultural traits, orientation and tradition.

Anthropologists have typically treated culture in a nominal manner as if it were some kind of boundable entity, a group, an organization of meaning and value that endures through time and that evolves according to its own internal logic—while ethnicity has remained somewhat of a sociological aspect, a process of intergroup identification and ascription, reference and boundary-maintenance.

Ethnicity is commonly associated with a chauvinistic kind of pride and ethnocentric essentialism—the ethnocentric pride in the superiority of one's own way of life over others, and, as well is commonly conflated with fallacious and fictitious ideologies of racial origins and biological superiority.

Much of modern ethnicity in state society as a common forum for resource interference and scramble competition, invites structural complementation of the rise of one group at the expense of others, and constitutes a kind of solution to the problem of open competition through structural hierarchy.

In such a context much that is "ethnic" about identity passes as fictitious, self-serving and fake vis-à-vis reference and counter-reference others. Ethnicity as state determined identity rather than ground-up ethnoculture becomes more essentialist and primordialist in social-symbolic rationalization and discriminating in asymmetric social relation and action than essential or actually necessary to the efficient ordering the state society as a whole if broader tolerance limits were in play.

States with high levels of cultural homogeneity may be mostly spared the problems chronic to radically plural societies, particularly those of a post-colonial background, even though no state in the modern world is completely free of this kind of often-focal socio-cultural dilemma.

Culture is typically treated as something that is more fundamental and basic to humankind, our social constructs and our identity complexes—it is social, it is universal, it is pervasive in all we do, it is largely out of awareness, and thus mostly transparent and invisible within ourselves.

And yet ethnos and culture cannot be effectively separated in our analysis of human reality, as neither can we tease out what are psychological variables, historical changes and continuities, and our own-shared constructions of reality.

Ethnos and Culture coexists along a common continuum, a continuum that is multidimensional and which is itself constituted by a complex relational dialectic between many mutually constraining factors and forces.

This ethno-cultural continuum exists through real historical time, across real social space—it only exists because all people, as actors upon the same stage, face a common dilemma in transacting and negotiating the boundaries and areas of their realities with other, different people, for the sake of continuity and perpetuity.

Ethnoculture then, is the study of how people, their identity, their social positions, their consciousness and outlook upon the world, are critically conditioned and constrained by their inevitable relationships with other peoples. It is a study of human difference, of how such difference can be constitutive of unity and diversity, cooperation and conflict, in the world.

Ethnoculture is also a study in how we become shaped by the many influences of the social world that we live within, and how, in turn we come to shape that world.

Finally, Ethnoculture is also a critically reflexive study of the relative limits of our knowledge of both others and of ourselves in the social world—just as we cannot clearly disentangle where the study of ethnos ends and the understanding of culture begins, so too we cannot finally say where ends the problematic understanding of ourselves and where begins the unproblematic study of others.

The understanding of Peranakan ethnoculture cannot be had outside of its broader "traditional" Southeast Asian context. It shares many of the continuities that are distinctive of Southeast Asian civilization.

Civilization is here taken to be a trans-cultural and panhuman process of historical development—a process that is socially and culturally integrative and interregional in scope.

Certain general cultural style-patterns are associated with particular instances of civilization, as are particular incidences of "Great Men" or people of genius whose innovativeness and spirit serve to characterize the style-pattern of the age.

The civilizing process consists of a structural dialectic of emergent complexity in interregional systems, a dialectic involving social, political, economic, religious and psychological factors.

It involves increasing levels and areas of integration and increasing heterogeneity of socio-cultural transmission from local to regional and interregional to even global contexts, that result in stimulus generation of modified patterns at all levels of human organization.

Processes of both exogenous, or external, acculturative influences of change, as well as internal, endogenous enculturative influences are involved in the construction and transmission of ethnoculture.

Peranakan ethnoculture as both part of a wider confluence of Southeast Asian Civilization and as constituting a particular culture historical instance of typical, and in some ways, prototypical, Southeast Asian civilization, is the product of many diverse extraneous influences. Thus, Peranakan culture has its place within broader cultural and historical streams of the human world that deserve closer study and understanding.

The Making of "Southeast Asia"

Southeast Asia remains one of the most heterogeneous, long settled, and most culturally, ethnically, racially, linguistically and historically complicated regions in the World.

Geographically, it has been conventionally divided between insular, or "Island Southeast Asia"— including Malaysia, Borneo, Singapore, Brunei, and the vast arc of island archipelagos including Indonesia and the Philippines—and peninsular, or Mainland Southeast Asia—including Thailand, Burma, Kampuchea, Laos and Vietnam—reflecting another important contrast in the region between the maritime orientation of the many miles of shoreline and the "mountain" orientation of the central highland chains and the major river systems and valleys (the Red River, the Mekong, the Chao Phraya, and the Irrawaddy, as well as the mighty Ganges system to the northwest.)

Strong culture historical reasons are sometimes given for including Sri Lanka, Assam, Yunnan, Hainan, Formosa and even New Guinea and Madagascar, although these political entities are conventionally peripheral to the region circumscribed by the designation of Southeast Asia.

There is a sense that words like Southeast Asia name both more and less than the reality they are held to designate— more are the hidden implications of power and asymmetry between the namer and the named; the less is the sense of "science fiction" that is created by the labeling process, the metaphorical allusions of exoticism, strangeness, and romance that accrete to such distant toponyms.

> "Thus in East and West alike the word 'Asia' is really an equivoque. It has no fixed meaning—no clear-cut denotation—but it is extraordinarily rich in emotional connotations. Though these make it the despair of the logician, they enhance its value for the poet, the artist— and the politician." (J. Steadman, The Myth of Asia, 1969: 35)

The term "Southeast Asia" leads to a reification and projection of a spurious sense of homogeneity, unity and boundedness onto the region it delimits on the globe, one that is actually as culturally diverse and complicated as it is historically entangled and unbounded.

Peranakan

The cross-roads of the Orient has long been a meeting place, and a region of cultural intermingling, between many different kinds of people, such that one will find anywhere one travels in Southeast Asia a profusion of different religions, ethnic identities, and cultural orientations within the same marketplace, within the same city limits, even under the same roof. Southeast Asia, from a regional perspective, becomes a veritable mosaic of human difference and variation.

There are common themes in Southeast Asian life that confers an overall unity to the diversity of life found there. "Unity in diversity" is the predominant theme of Southeast Asian Studies.

A vegetable culture, a bamboo culture, a rice and fish culture, a monsoon culture, a riverine culture—Southeast Asia can be characterized by its commonly shared characteristics which have helped to shape its life-ways.

But also recurrent in the region are other general themes—

- The importance of maritime trade.
- The importance of jungle products and trade
- The chameleon kind of identity.
- The relatively high status of women.
- The dialectical tension between the peoples of the highlands and the people of the lowlands.
- The role that both great religions and indigenous animism and spirituality has always played in the daily life of its people.
- The proximity and cultural appreciation of the natural world.
- The unifying role that the rivers and streams have long played in the integration of its areas.
- The outward looking orientation of its people.

- The periodic waves of acculturative change that have occasionally swept through the region.
- The dialectical push and pull between autochthonous and heterochthonous origins.
- The deep sense of cyclical, rhythmical time of ancient, traditional civilizations.

Such common themes amount to no more than the reiteration of trite truisms whose substantive basis is not apparent until one has lived and traveled within Southeast Asia among Southeast Asians.

In claiming that the Southeast Asian setting, it's nature, its geography, its climate, has had an important shaping influence upon Southeast Asian culture and character is to risk falling back into an old argument about environmental determinism.

But the influence is there, and has been remarked upon in reference to:

- The use of space and geographical orientation among the Balinese.
- The ritual ecologies of New Guinea highlanders or the Rhade of the Vietnamese highlands.
- The thematic recurrence of nature symbolism in Vietnamese literature and poetry, art and music.
- The spiritual animism of the Dayaks of Borneo.
- The cultural ecologies of highlanders throughout the region.
- The ecology of rice among the Thais and the Javanese, and other lowlanders throughout all of Southeast Asia, etc.

Many other examples can be found to attest to the direct symbolic role and value that nature and the natural environment has played in influencing the aesthetic sensitivities and religious sensibilities of the peoples of Southeast Asia, whether this is in the religion, arts and music, festivals and cuisines, architecture, and other trades and crafts.

Perhaps it is because nature in this tropical setting is so intrusive in virtually every part of one's life—whether it is:

— An everyday morning parade of ants through the halls, over the walls, and across the ceilings of one's home,
— Or a resident "*chi chak*" in one's kitchen sink or six inch long centipede in one's outhouse sink,
— Or the encroaching jungle growth that appears in every crack of the sidewalk,
— Or the torrents of rain that fall endlessly from the high clouds,
— Or the monitor lizard in the parking lot of a major university and the other smaller ones that live in the drain pipes of one's yard,
— Or the flitting fruit bats attacking the Mango tree in the late evening.

One cannot easily escape the direct contact with nature that living in a Southeast Asian setting brings.

Not all Southeast Asians are equally and unequivocally lovers of nature or conscientious conservationists of the region's natural resources—irreversible destruction of many primeval forest habitats continues at a ceaseless and alarming rate.

Many people in their daily activities and attitudes evince little concern or appreciation of their natural environment. And yet many of the most basic cultural patterns that predominate in Southeast Asia can be found to have direct linkages with the natural tropical habitat.

What is commonly referred to in the literature as the traditional, interregional system of Southeast Asian civilization, must be seen as a structurally and socially persistent patterns, constrained by its ball and chain mountain, maritime and tropical cultural geography, of the <u>organization of diversity</u>—diversity that is ecological, economic and ethnic.

The principle of ethnos lies at the base of Southeast Asian cultural identity. Social organization based upon such a principle of ethnos, is characteristically of a "plural" and culturally heterogeneous society. Indeed, the concept of ethnic "pluralism" was coined by J. S. Furnival in reference to Southeast Asia (British Colonial Burma).

D. E. Brown; (<u>Principles of Social Structure</u>, 1976) notes seven conditions necessary for the maintenance of radically plural societies that are typical of Southeast Asian settings:

1. Continuity of stable economic and ecological conditions within and between regions (Ibid, pg. 82).

2. Relative isolation of the radically plural society from other similar sized but differently structured societies (Ibid, pg. 85-6).

3. Demographic ratios between ruling and rule maintained or changed in favor of the ruling elite (Ibid, pg. 86).

4. Social identities and boundaries maintained by stereotypically generalizing differences across all spheres—religious, familial, educational, occupational, economic, etc.—thus restricting inter-group acculturation and mobility (Ibid, pg. 87).

5. Symbiotic relations offering primary compensations for the subordinate minority and religious or ideological orientations offering deferred compensations are encouraged (Ibid, pg. 88).

6. The corporate exclusiveness, superior organization, solidarity and cohesion of the ruling group should be systematically promoted (Ibid, pg. 88).

7. Authority should be sacralized and legitimized by an inclusive cult offering compensation in another life or advocating withdrawal from worldly affairs. (Ibid, pg. 90).

The basic model of corporate social structure based upon the principle of ethnos implied by this formal paradigm is held to characterize the developmental dynamics of typically Southeast Asian civilization from its first prehistoric inception perhaps as long ago as several thousands of years until today.

It is a model in which numerous, relatively homogenous, local groups came into increasing contact with one another, and with extra-regional peoples, and in the resulting processes of intercultural contact and transmission, there developed increasing levels of heterogeneity and socio-structural complexity.

This model is held to be critically linked to the development of the economic exploitation of the entire region, and the emergence of an increasingly complex interregional system, based upon commerce and hinterland exploitation, in which local people were to become increasingly integrated and more culturally sophisticated and cosmopolitan.

Civilization is thus also held to be a developmental process of interregional integration, represented by increasing levels of complexity of socio-political organization, increasing economic integration and exploitation, and the increasing influence of religious ideas and orientations upon the social organization.

The Nanyang Network

Of course, the history of the so-called "Straits Settlements," in which the Baba's are mostly associated, is but one small chapter, one small part of the total Southeast Asian tapestry.

These settlements, including Singapore, Malacca, Penang, as well as the major port and inland cities of Java, are the principle centers for the development of Baba and Peranakan culture, which spread outwardly into the hinterland regions of the various provinces of peninsular Malaysia and insular Indonesia.

The Chinese presence in Southeast Asia, or what is known among the Chinese as the South Sea, or Nanyang, dates back to before Christ. Long present in the Southeast Asian setting, they have long been there as merchants, travelers, ex-patriots seeking refuge.

The Chinese of the Nanyang have long been the classic "sojourning entrepreneurs" seeking their fortunes in foreign lands. Sojourning involved migration of men and remittances of money back to the homeland—the Overseas Chinese, no matter how far they traveled or how long away, never really forgot their original ties back in their homeland—among the Nanyang Chinese it also involved local, overseas organization for the mobilization of men, resources, capital and money.

> "The sojourning pattern is found centuries back in Asia within China, between China and Southeast Asia, and within Southeast Asia..." (John T. Omohundro, "Trading Pattern of Philippine Chinese: Strategies of Sojourning

Peranakan

> Middlemen, in <u>Economic Exchange and Social Interaction inSoutheastAsia</u>1977: 113-4).

Long present in Southeast Asia, perhaps as early as the first century AD, and certainly by the fifth, the early Chinese communities were considered 'transient' and not well organized. Enough archaeological evidence suggests they had early, far reaching trade networks.

Early Nanyang contacts in Southeast Asia were primarily colonial, mercantile and maritime. Undoubtedly many of these first sojourners were also "pirate-traders" issuing from the sea-coasts and many islands of southeastern China, the coastline of East China, the islands of the China Sea and the Island of Taiwan (Formosa), as well as also being a part of the regular southward bound excess and push of human population thrown off by perennial political turmoil in the central and northern provinces and counties of the "Great Agrarian State" (Mainland China).

Political and social pressures beginning far to the North in China had long had a rippling effect that stimulated an ever-southward movement of Chinese and their civilization. When their march southward reached the South China Sea, they found land routes cut off to their further advance. There remained but the Nanyang trade, later fueled by a form of debt indenture, and a credit-ticket system.

These same people took to the seas in expanding economic, versus territorial, frontiers. The closing of the southern borders with the newly won independence of Vietnam in the Ninth Century, AD, and the gradual shift of commerce from Haiphong to the major port cities of Southeastern China, led to a growing maritime exodus and exchange of Chinese peoples over the whole of the Nanyang.

Subsequent periods of migration of Nanyang Chinese are considered like "waves" that fanned out from Southeastern and Eastern China that swept across the entire Southeast Asian region and beyond.

From the Tang and Sung Dynastic periods, circa the Seventh through the Tenth Centuries, in which foreign trade in China became a more important source of revenue, there is an emergence of a somewhat separate and distinct merchant class—a successful and wealthy bourgeoisie that did not fit into the traditional Chinese Mandarin-based social system.

The design and construction of more sea-worthy, deep-draft junks allowed the Chinese to venture further afield from the coastlines to which they had previously clung so closely. This phase represented the early "tribute-bearing/junk-trade" missions that helped to establish Chinese political authority, as distant as it was, as well as to secure much-prized exotic trade goods.

This period most notably climaxed with the voyages of Imperial Eunuch *Cheng Ho*, who in command of a fleet of more than sixty large junks carrying more than thirty-thousand soldiers, resulting in the conquest of many kingdoms, establishment of Imperial Chinese influence and presence in the Nanyang, as well as in the founding of the trading port of Malacca in 1408.

The next phase of Chinese activity in the Nanyang is linked to the political ascendancy of the Manchus over the Ming Dynasty—the "contact period" is marked by the introduction of European interests in the region, inaugurated by the capture of Malacca by the Portuguese only one hundred years after its founding, and cumulatively increasing foreign (Dutch, French and British) competition for control over the region.

Official Chinese interest in the Nanyang was withdrawn, and Chinese immigration to the Nanyang was even banned under penalty of execution. Thus, Chinese subsequently migrating to the Nanyang, from the Mid-Seventeenth until the early Nineteenth Centuries, were those who were politically oriented away from Manchu China, and who sought refuge in the Chinese communities of the Nanyang.

Many Chinese villages and Chinatowns today throughout Southeast Asia bear many "survival" traits of a by-gone Ming Dynasty era, in typical Chinese conservatism and ritualistic form little altered several centuries later.

Though European domination in Southeast Asia subordinated the role of the Chinese, it opened up new and lucrative niches for economic development in expanding colonial markets, and stimulated new waves of economic migration to the Nanyang that the Europeans hardly controlled, and in some cases, even promoted through policies and actions.

The Chinese, as a pariah class, provided an important linkage in the articulation of the colonial system of resource exploitation—they became the inveterate merchant-middlemen/money-lenders. As such Nanyang Chinese came to specialize as "pariah Capitalists" in the articulation of local to regional to world economies.

They became agricultural pioneers of the tropical frontiers, miners, small planters, and overseers. They came to occupy the middle positions of the colonial administrative apparatus. They were also the source of a bottomless supply of cheap coolie labor, easily mobilizable, transportable, and extremely adaptable to adverse environments and difficult circumstances.

Among the Chinese, a veritable Nanyang empire developed—a vast network through which the movement of labor, finance, capital and commerce was facilitated by a wide range of interlinked exchange agencies and agents at every level and in every niche of the Southeast Asian setting.

The relative mobility of "capital and labor increases Chinese responsiveness to market fluctuations, allowing them to bail out quickly from failures and capitalize fully on fleeting opportunities." (John T. Omohundro, 1977:117)

The Nanyang of this period continued to prosper in the area of trade and finance to the point that it gained virtual monopolies over many sectors and areas of the Southeast Asian interregional economy—particularly rice and metal. Many of their practices were extremely exploitative, and their success at the hands of European colonists was often strongly resented by indigenous peoples.

As Nanyang civilization developed and grew more economically integrated, its agents grew increasingly situated by and entangled within local arrangements and became increasingly unable to uproot themselves in order to return to China.

The line between sojourning and actual colonization was thus thin—as the ties to the homeland grew distant and were severed, the Chinese who found themselves locally and regionally entangled within the Nanyang network, reoriented their outlook and attitude toward their local Southeast Asian context. The first thing they did was to send for their wives and children from China. First, brothers joined brothers, then "sisters" began increasingly to come and settle in Southeast Asia.

The sex ratios of the Chinese communities, always male-biased, became stabilized by the late 19th Century, and this tended to stabilize the community, its Chinese identity and the "transience" within it.

The increasing presence of Chinese women in the Nanyang reversed the trend toward intermarriage with local people and led to the formation of a Chinese community that maintained its separate biological and cultural identity—Nanyang Civilization, as a typically "Overseas Chinese" cultural orientation, became more "complete" (Yen Ching-Hwang, 1986)

The Twentieth Century, modernization, and especially World War II, brought a change in the position of the Nanyang in Southeast Asia, but not an end to its economic monopolization and empire. New Nationalisms throughout Southeast Asia supported structural policies of enforced assimilation, systematic discrimination, ethnization, and even political persecution and periodic mass mobilization of native populations against the Chinese minorities of the Nanyang.

In some aspects the Nanyang empire has been slowly melting, or eroding under the gradual, long-term impetus of these policies. But the Chinese, and their position in the Southeast Asian economy, has proven difficult to replace.

Crucial to the historical background of the Straits Settlements has been the larger context of the so-called "Nanyang"—the Overseas "Imperio in Imperium", or "Empire within an Empire." It extended southeastward from the Southeast Coastline of China, throughout Southeast Asia, stretching across the Polynesian Pacific to eventually encompass the New World, as well as along the Imperial pathways of the British Commonwealth, eventually spreading its net even into the Caribbean and further abroad.

The extensiveness of this economic empire is to be matched only by its subterranean character, the entrepreneurial efficacy and savvy of its agents, and the strength of social ties that have so effectively held it together through more than a century and a half of marginalization, persecution, discrimination, hardship and struggle.

A gigantic iceberg—it rears its tiny head above the surface of the Pacific only in Singapore, Macau and Hong Kong. Long a two-headed dragon, it is soon to become only a single entity—Singapore—a strange feudalistic anachronism in a modern age of political capitalism and economic imperialism; a mercantile city-state; an island unto itself at the very tip of the Eurasian continent. But its influence is still strongly felt in almost every country bordering the Pacific, and in many beyond.

In many respects representative of the unique cultural stylizations of the Nanyang world, the place and rise of the Babas as a distinctive cultural orientation, more than any other single factor, must be fit within the framework of the development of Nanyang civilization—in many respects representative of the unique cultural stylizations of the Nanyang world. However Malayanized the Babas might have become, they remained importantly, and distinctively, Chinese in orientation.

It would serve well to briefly compare and contrast Nanyang culture and ethnicity with Baba ethnoculture. As an empire, the Nanyang is interregional, and incorporates a wide arc of humanity beneath its broad umbrella. Singapore has become the exclusive capital city of this empire, the central core of its civilization, and Singapore has also always been one of the principle places of the original Straits Settlements of the Babas and Nonyas.

The Babas, with their Western orientation, were the original pioneers of Singapore. They became the traditional ruling elite of the capital of the Nanyang, and it is in this way that the Baba culture has come to serve, somewhat ambivalently and ambiguously as an indirect cultural model for Nanyang civilization.

But not all citizens of the Nanyang are or were Babas—most were not—and the Baba has been in the contemporary epoch a dying breed though important remnants of the Baba orientation remain with a strong Chinese identity, a Western outlook focused upon the British model, as well as accompanied by strong ties to a local Southeast Asia cultural setting. What has been lost mostly from this orientation has been the Malayanized aspects that gave it a distinctive flavor and style in the first place.

A model of the function of ethnos in the decision-making process of migration, identity and development that goes into the history of the making of Nanyang civilization is evident from the consideration of Baba culture in the larger context of the Nanyang—the Babas were a kind of pariah class created through cultural integration, acculturation, and amalgamation between Muslim Malays and Buddhist Chinese, in which basic differences in religious tenets precluded the kind of complete cultural assimilation that became possible in Thailand.

Post-Independence Malaysia fostered strict policies of structural discrimination and segregation between the Malays and the Chinese—these policies led to the disintegration of the basis of Baba culture. Singapore, a Chinese city, gained its own independence from Malaysia, and, in the definition of its newfound national identity, excluded all that was Malay from its own identity.

Those aspects of Baba culture that were Malay were cast out, leaving a gulf in its identity between the East and the West. At first it strongly oriented itself to the British model, and later has gone through a period of re-Sinicization in developmental focus upon Chinatowns, renewing trade contacts with Taiwan, and increasingly, with Mainland China.

The situation for the Baba's of Malacca was just the reverse. The oldest Baba community, and in many respects the most Malayanized, these people found themselves symbolically appropriated and at the same time enclaved as the museum pieces of Malaysian national heritage.

They have since come to represent the archetypical Babas, though they were but a variant of a more general theme. These Babas had no option in the matter but to submit to their own cultural cooption by the Malays.

In Penang, the next oldest Baba settlement, which remains more than 90% Chinese in composition, the pathway taken by the Baba communities was a bit more tragic.

These Babas strongly identified with the British, and were less Malayan than the Malacca Chinese. They initiated a separatist movement for Penang's status, similar to Singapore, but failed, not receiving the backing by the British.

Ethnos can be seen as a principle determinant factor in the decisions and opportunities open to people in the course of their lives. People attempt to optimize their prospects, given alternative sets of possibilities, but these possibilities themselves are constrained within a larger, ethnically defined context, such that choices made are not unlimited, and vary considerably for different peoples.

The Nanyang can be seen as a vast network of crisscrossing pathways that allowed labor, resources and capital to move in different, frequently shifting, directions.

Against systematic discrimination or persecution, Chinese were and remain faced with a range of alternative choices—

they can either opt to assimilate completely into the local population, become enclaved and ghettoized, segregated and discriminated against, or else migrate back to China or seek and relocate to a new homeland in another part of the Nanyang or further abroad to the Chinese diaspora, to Commonwealth communities, the U.S., or to other diaspora Chinatowns around the world.

The flight of Capital from Hong Kong to the U.S., the Nanyang and the Commonwealth, is but one more example of this social historical movement of people, wealth, resources and culture.

Which directions Chinese took depended partly upon the dialect group—Cantonese will take Cantonese pathways, and Hokkien will follow Hokkien roads. Not all Chinese of the Nanyang hold Singaporean culture to be the model or principle orientation of their lives.

Increasingly, many of the offspring of a Baba population, estimated at near 8 million souls worldwide, have made their way further afield such that we can speak of a "Peranakan diaspora" only partially overlapping with the other mainly Chinese diaspora communities. Many have been carried abroad around the world in pursuit of professional careers, work contracts, interracial marriages, schooling and business.

The Singaporeans have, by and large, been cut from their roots to the Chinese homeland, but many Chinese throughout the Nanyang, Malaysia included, have maintained these Ancestral ties for generations.

Chinese may see Singapore symbolically as a success story, as a financial capital and trade center of the Nanyang, but they do not identify with the Anglicized, modernized Baba orientation of the Singaporean people—they look elsewhere for their models of Chinese-ness.

The principle virtue and limitation of the Baba people are that they no longer live directly under their Ancestor's shadow. Singaporean culture is native to Singapore and the Straits, and this is their homeland to which they are fixed.

Chinese who have kept their ties to the mainland have other options open to them, but do not see Singapore or Singaporean culture as the primary alternative for their lives.

The virtue of the larger Nanyang identity that depends upon its old identification with the mainland is that this permits the Chinese a relatively wide access to a number of possible alternatives—Chinese become united under a broader umbrella of pan-Chinese-ness which encompasses different dialect groups.

Such Chinese are permitted to work together and even trust one another in contexts in which the only common bond may be a superficial knowledge of Mandarin. This latitude is an advantage of maintaining a Nanyang orientation not permitted to the Babas.

The principle of the cultural models of ethnos in providing options and in constraining the directions of decision-making in peoples' lives is an important one. We can see that such ethnos is always defined vis-à-vis reference or counter-reference groups—for the Singaporeans, the Malays are a counter-reference other, and constitute the greatest threat to their separate identity.

On the other hand, the British model has served as the principle reference group for these peoples. Other models are available to other Chinese—some may still look to the mainland, others to the Nationalist Government of Taiwan.

Peranakan

Many undoubtedly see their successful cousins in the United States and the Commonwealth. Many are likely to follow those who went before them.

Perhaps the greatest illusion that a Westerner could entertain with regard to the Chinese is that they are all basically the same. The very basis of ethnic Chinese identity is its crosscutting "nesting" of identities within a larger network of social distinctions on the basis of village, clan, kin-group, dialect, class, age, etc.

Every Chinese has a place within the vast theater, and every Chinese is supposed to know this place. Indeed, ethnos, or ethnicity, for the ethnic Chinese, is the primary organizational principle of their society. Chinese typically draw fine distinctions between other Chinese that are invisible to Non-Chinese eyes.

Intra-ethnic Chinese distinctions have been referred to as "sub-ethnic" identities based upon local-linguistic-ethnic distinctions. It is highly ascriptive, automatic and somewhat obligatory in character, being linked to the strong patrilineal reckoning of Chinese kinship.

Chinese successfully exploited this organizational ethos of ethnos in navigating and negotiating several different status-role identities within more than one organizational structure. They thrive on a fundamental status ambiguity, inter-positioning between structures, and a kind of Chameleon-ness of cultural linguistic code switching that would befuddle most others.

Chinese may well be one big family, but it is a family well divided under one roof. The terminological distinctions made in kinship reckoning are fine and of massive detail. It is fitting that both Chinese Heaven and Hell are vast multi-tiered bureaucratic structures occupied by greater and lesser gods.

Clan organization and a segmentary lineage structure facilitate mobilization as well as fine-tuning of internal differentiations. Trade associations, secret societies, Kong sis, all cross-cut clan and lineage structures to weave Chinese into a closely-knit social clothe, often well under official radars.

II: The Birth of the Babas

The Babas of Malaysia and Singapore and the Peranakan of Indonesia share a common kind of Creole orientation in a local and regional context. Their communities constitute local variations upon a shared cultural continuum, the limits and dimensionality of which are, broadly speaking, the function of a style of accommodation and a kind of broader pattern of acculturation.

These communities all share basic, derivative and distinctive cultural correlates within a similar, regionally defined culture-historical framework, which can be treated in a comparative manner and can be used as a relative index of cultural distance and difference, acculturative influence, cultural change and continuity, as well as the basis for the construction of a hypothetical, prototypical ethnocultural and ethno-historical baseline by which a broader, deeper culture historical understanding can be derived.

Issues of ethnoculture and ethno-history cannot be clearly separated, especially in regard to such groups as the Babas and Nonyas whose social organization, ethnic identity, history, and culture appear to be inextricably interrelated in such a way that we cannot analytically separate out for study one dimension without becoming entangled in all the other dimensions of study.

An attempt to write an ethno-historiography in recognition of these inherent complexities constitutes an attempt to combine stylistic elements of ethnographic description and ethnological explanation with other stylistic elements of historiographical narrative and chronology, as well as an attempt to effectively integrate macroscopic dimensions of culture historical and political economic proportions with microscopic dimensions of human participants making human decisions and mistakes in everyday situations.

In this regard, the key linkage is held to be the effective context of the small group network—at which level of analysis individual decision-making becomes bound to and critically constrained by small group-dynamics, values, group incentives and cultural constraints.

Such small, sub-cultural groupings are not strictly molecular in their structural organization—they are cellular in possessing semi-permeable boundaries and osmotic qualities that allow a certain amount and kind of crossing over. These boundaries are defined, refined and revised in relation to other such groupings, to individuals' reference points, and to larger social contexts of participation and historical events.

They are symbolic as well, being more the nature of maze-ways and maps, passageways, doors and keys, defined by elements of language, nonverbal communication, social positionality, worldview, cultural orientation and models, which individuals learn to navigate their relationships with different people. Such boundaries are rarely static and are always socially, psychologically and culture historically dynamic. They are negotiated, transformed, maintained, etc., through our ongoing interrelation with others.

Ethnicity has come to encompass a variety of different meanings—ethnos, ethnic identity, classification, ethnic studies, ethnogeny, the nexus of "race, culture, ethnic groupings and nationalities," as structuralist "ethnic boundaries" rooted in "eco-niches", competitive exclusion for resources, social or material, social stratification, ethno-religious value orientation, and ethno-political ideology and ethnic group organization and mobilization.

There is intrinsic to the understanding of ethnicity created in plural social settings, including: the notion of ethnarchy, or ethnic stratification of communally ordered societies involving unequal "majority/minority" relations; presence and reinforcement and interaction of ethno-classes; hierarchical class/caste stratification across ethnic lines; unequal institutional deformations and practices; internal/external colonization of groups; as well as embedded and opportunistic social and structural patterns of ethnic-based or social discrimination.

All this may occur systematically or informally within an interregional or world systems framework that defines structural and social asymmetries between core, semi-periphery and peripheral regions.

There are also acculturation perspectives that deal with analytical problems of social integration, amalgamation, assimilation and accommodation as well as problems of transmission, mobility, and stratification.

Then there is labeling theory, which focuses upon the foundation and effects of ethnic stereotyping and labeling in maintaining social distance, thresholds and barriers between groups. A symbolic approach views the ethno-historical repository and revitalization of symbols of ethnic identity and ethnic group solidarity, which may be used differentially in different periods and places to configure and reconfigure identities of difference and sameness.

A Marxist theory of "ethnikos" defines an ethnic community, "or ethos in a narrow sense of the word", "as a historically formed aggregate of people who share common, relatively stable specific features of culture (including language) and psychology, realization of their unity and distinctiveness from other similar aggregates of people as well as the self-nomination." (Yu V. Bromley, <u>On the Typology of Ethnic Communities</u>, 1978: 18)

Ethnikos is not an isolated phenomenon, but occurs in a nexus of several levels of social institutionalization "from family to state." "The combination of ethnic properties with social properties as such depends, to a certain extent, on the spatial parameters of ethnikos, on a compact or scattered distribution of the bearers of ethnic properties themselves." (Bromley, 1978: pg. 18)

This definition of ethnikos fits the general problem of ethnicity within a larger political economic and social systems framework. Immanuel Wallerstein does not distinguish between "nations, nationalities, peoples, ethnic groups," but all these terms "denote variants of a single phenomenon" which he refers to as "ethno-nations" which are identifiable by their articulatory function within the world economy as a whole.

We may extend and modify this thesis somewhat to say that such ethnikos fits within variable levels of familial, local, provincial, state, regional, interregional and global systems, all of which are interrelated. Ethnikos must always be framed within a larger structure of social interaction—ethnic analysis must take into account the relative positioning, and inter-positionality of both individuals and communities within these different systemic levels.

Immanuel Wallerstein distinguishes between ranges of interest and interaction within the core, periphery and semi-periphery. "The meaning of ethnic consciousness in a core area is considerably different from that of ethnic consciousness in a peripheral area precisely because of the different class positions such ethnic groups have in a world economy." (I. Wallerstein, The Capitalist World Economy, 1979:pg. 24-5)

The ethnic identity of the Overseas Chinese of Southeast Asia is within a semi-peripheral social position, in which consciousness is "inter-class" and therefore inherently ambiguous in its relative juxtaposition between core and periphery.

From the perspective of the periphery, it shares features of the core. From the standpoint of the core, it shares aspects of the periphery. Structurally and socially, therefore, the ethnic status identity of the Chinese of the Nanyang is inherently ambivalent and problematic, an ambiguity that reverberates upon all levels of its articulatory functioning.

The problematic function and dilemma of this ethnic consciousness is to span and effectively resolve this dilemma. We may refer to this as a process of ethnization—as a mode of social production, as an ideological mode of information, and as a dialectical mode of "ethnic realization."

It is an open-ended historical process in its extension, and reapplication to historically situated and particular phenomena, and thus accretes new meanings and a transformational base for its growth and development as a distinctive ethno-cultural phenomenon.

It becomes a referential and organizational metaphor as well—realities and issues become ethnicized when cast in the terminology of an "ethnical language game." Ethnic groups, boundaries, identities and categories become, to some extent, phenomena of reification that the researcher takes part in reinforcing—such reified ideas and words then take a life and history of their own.

We must also refer to an ethnic style or stylization that is distinctive and culture historically unique, and that may also be quite adaptive in functional integration within a given social context.

We must see the process of ethnization and stylization from both an etic and emic point of view, as dialectically interdependent and systematic, and involving processes that are both endogenous and exogenous, internal and external, in origin and orientation.

Ethnarchy carries the connotation of hierarchy within a communalistic framework—stratification that has structurally variable social, psychological, political, economic, religious and cultural dimensions and consequences—that may be expressed or emphasized differentially in the process of ethnization.

Furthermore, ethnarchy in ethnization also implies a process of colonial institutionalization, or 'colonization"—implying the function of "social distance" in the political control of identity and practice primarily for economic interests and intentions. Social distance as a mechanism for ethnic stratification also involves the notion of group 'boundary' maintenance.

Interethnic conflict and political violence in Malaysia between Chinese and Malays can be seen as an effective smoke-screen for the maintenance of intra-group vertical stratification, and for the protection and promotion of the interests and prerogatives of an exclusive elite on both sides of the coin.

There is a hidden "elite-mass" dimension to the communal policies and politics of ethnic difference. Economically, as defined by the class relations of a common marketplace, a hierarchy of interests is effectively masked by ethnic stratification. The existential realities of both Chinese and Malays are rooted in the same economic dilemmas of underdevelopment and structural poverty.

Political power and economic advantage exist in a socio-structural dialectic—access to resources, opportunities, skills and incentives underlie empowerment and political organization—and political legitimacy and mobilization in turn decisively determines and critically conditions economic change, development and differential access to resources.

In Nanyang social structure, the path to leadership lay through social influence obtained through economic achievement and acquisition. Political privilege in turn increases wealth and prestige. "The circle was complete..." (John Chin, The Sarawak Chinese, 1981: 79)

From the standpoint of the structural efficacy of power, ethnic labels "conceal the underlying struggle for the appropriation of certain economic, political, and social advantages among the different racial and status groups in the wider Malaysian society...(Lawrence K. L. Siaw, The Legacy of Malaysian Chinese Social Structure, 1981)

As merchant middlemen, the Chinese were focused upon the Southeast Asian marketplace and market economy. They came to depend upon what Max Weber has called the critical market "moment" of class advantage in the buying and selling of commodities. As such, they were a marginal minority, articulating and mediating different levels of the political-economic structure of Southeast Asian society.

Their place within a developing Southeast Asian context was pivotal—existing for purposes of social stability and for buffering of conflict-laden tensions between core and periphery, elite and masses.

The Nanyang Chinese were both bought off from the top, and became the social scapegoats for tension from the bottom—the Overseas Chinese as a community is therefore caught in the classic dilemma of the double-bind, depending for its very ethnic identity on structural processes and positions that threaten that identity and its socio-political security.

It becomes both exploiter and exploited, without political legitimacy or independence. It has been a commercial-urban middle-stratum containing and resisting social pressures towards social integration and homogenization, in a marginally discontinuous position rendering them constantly vulnerable to conflict or confiscation.

Baba Beginnings

The Babas of Malaysia commonly referred to themselves as Peranakan, and even though among Malays this may have had derogative connotations of "mixed" or impure blood, the Baba's were proud of their heritage and of their name. John Clammer notes that Peranakan "is the Malay designation for 'local-born people'" (<u>Straits Chinese Society</u>1980: pg. 3)

According to Tan Giok-San who wrote the first comprehensive ethnography of the Peranakan of Indonesia, the word "Peranakan" is derived from the Malayo-Indonesian root "*anak*", meaning child, with the prefix "per" and suffix "an", rendering the meaning "born of" (<u>The Chinese of Sukabumi</u> 1963: pg. 11).

In modern medical terminology, "Peranakan" is the part of the female anatomy closely describing the uterus. (Wazir Jahan Karim, "Prelude to Madness: The Language of Emotion in Courtship and Early Marriage" in <u>Emotions of Culture: A Malay Perspective</u>, edited by Wazir Jahan Karim, 1990:49)

Peranakan

"Malay midwives describe it as the place in the abdomen where 'the foetus clings' and the baby begins to grow. Hence it is closely associated with blood, semen and fertilization, in the sense that a foetus is recognized to develop from a clot of blood after fertilization takes place." (Ibid. pg. 49-50)

Peranakan Indonesia or Peranakan Malaysia refers to "born of Indonesia" or "born of Malaysia" respectively. It came to have the euphemistic connotation of "mixed-blood" and was applied to any native-born who were of mixed descent—Arab Peranakan, Chinese Peranakan, Dutch Peranakan, Jawi Peranakan, etc. It seems as though the Chinese Peranakan, always a significant, if not a preponderant, minority, appropriated the term as their own.

The terms Baba and Nonya (or Nonya or Nona,) are often applied to the Peranakan, particularly of the Straits Settlements. These terms mean "Man" or "Mister" and "Woman" or "Mrs." or "Miss," and carry the connotation of "Gentleman" and "Lady."

Again, according to Tan, Indonesian kin-terms used by elderly women, referring to the child's spouse, were sexually marked—"*Babah mantu*" (Daughter's husband) and "*Njonja mantu*" (Son's wife) (Tan Giok-lan, The Chinese of Sukabumi 1963: pg. 125). One can only speculate whether the terms Baba and Nonya became marked for those of mixed marriage between Chinese and Malayo-Indonesians, and thus appropriated by the Peranakan to refer to the male and female spouses of such marriages.

J. D. Vaughn, in his early work The Manners and Customs of the Chinese of the Straits Settlements (1879) traces the etymology of the word "Baba" as the a term used by Bengali descendants to designate European children, "and it is probable that the word was applied by the Indian convicts at

Pinang to Chinese children and so came into general use."
(Reprint, 1971: 2)

R. J. Wilkinson held that Baba was a descriptive name for
"European, Eurasian and Chinese males to distinguish them
from men born in Europe and China", and "Descriptive name
applied to male Straits-born Chinese."(R. J. Wilkinson, <u>A
Malay-English Dictionary</u>, 1959: 50)

Kobayashi Shinsaku has speculated that Baba may have
been a corruption of the Malay word for father, *Bapa*,
employed as an honorific for the Peranakan of Java.
(Kobayashi Shinsaku, <u>Shina Minzoku no Kaigai Hatten
Kakyo no Kenkyo</u>, 1931: 93)

John Clammer cites speculation that "Baba" should be
rendered as "*ba-ba,*" indicating ignorance of Chinese
language and customs. "If this is at all true, it would account
for many Straits Chinese disliking the term when it is applied
to them!" (1980, footnote, pg. 5)

On the other hand, Png Poh-Seng notes that: "In the heyday
of Straits Chinese prestige and influence, it was an
advantage to be a Baba, and it is not far-fetched to assume
that all Straits-born Chinese then liked to be known as
Babas." ("The Straits Chinese In Singapore" in <u>The Journal
of Southeast Asian History</u>, 1969:pg. 97)

Png Poh-Seng concurs with the early definition provided by
the Rev. Carstairs Douglas, "as it is fairly certain from
accounts of Sino-Malay marriages in Malacca that the term
was introduced to describe the progeny of such mixed
parentage." (Ibid, 1969: pg. 96)

Png Poh-Seng notes that "It was also not uncommon for
families, especially local-born *Tieochiu*, to name their sons
Tua-ba..., Ji-ba..., San-ba..., Si-ba..., and their daughters

Peranakan

Tua-nya..., *Ji-nya...*, *San-nya...*, and *Si-nya...*, in order of age." (Ibid. 1969: pg. 98)

My wife, a direct descendent of the Nonyas from Penang, sometimes sings to our baby girl "*Noni, noni keng, Ah pek jeep pang keng, pang keng mui bey key so, Ah pek long toe*" (translated, it reads "*Noni, noni keng*, old man goes into the bedroom, forgot bedroom door is not locked, the old man pushes it down.")

I ask her what the terms "*Noni, noni keng*" stand for, and where she first learned it, and she says she doesn't know, it just rhymes with the rest of the song, and it is something she had been singing since she was a child.

As grandmother of her first grandson, from the first day forward of his birth she began calling him little "Baba" which soon became "Ba" for short, with "Baba" being reserved for emphasis and sometimes indirect reference, almost as if his given formal name.

Excessive ink spilt over the speculative etymology of such words as Baba and Nonya and Peranakan is not mere equivocation, as it points up a fundamental dimension of ambiguity of such primary terms of reference—an ambiguity that is carried over into the other appellations, such as "Straits-Born" and "Straits Chinese" that is frequently used synonymously.

The British Rev. Carstairs Douglas, in his dictionary of spoken Amoy Hokkien, notes that the term "Baba" carried over into the Hokkien language to refer to "a half-caste Chinese from the Straits." In the Straits, however, the term is applied to all Chinese born there, half-caste or not." (J. D. Vaughn; 1879: pg. 2)

John Clammer again comments that: "there was from a very early date a distinction between the Straits Chinese, who were culturally distinct, and the other immigrant Chinese in the Straits Settlements"(1979, pg. 4).

The fundamental ambiguity found in all three sets of terms, Peranakan, Baba and Nonya, and Straits Chinese, is one of implicit denotative/connotative significance of "local born/mixed-blood," respectively.

Not all local born Chinese were half-caste or half-breed, even though they may or may not have been called "Peranakan", Baba, or Straits Chinese, and, at least for the Indonesian Peranakan, about three-quarters were of mixed parentage.

This ambiguity is essential to understanding the identity of the Peranakan and Babas, because they constituted an interstitial group situated somewhere between the Chinese and the Malayo-Indonesians, along two separate but convergent dimensions—racial and kinship identity, on the one hand, and, on the other hand, cultural and social identity and status.

It was just this between-ness, so important in-group and individual reference, that became linguistically "marked" by such special appellatives and that connotes ethnic pride or euphemistically in a derogative way to register cultural/racial inferiority.

The connotation of "native" or local-born seems more positively salient than the meaning of 'half-breed' that carries a negative connotation. Probably both sets of connotations were working simultaneously in highlighting the inherent ambiguity and ambivalence of fundamental "half-caste" identity.

———————

Peranakan

Some of the earliest evidence for the Chinese in the
Nanyang comes from archaeological sites in Java, Sumatra,
and Borneo, including Chinese sepulchral pottery vessels
that dated to the Second and First Centuries BCE. "From
these finds, De Flines inferred, no doubt correctly, that
Chinese colonists or merchants must have lived in Indonesia
as early as the Han period." (Victor Purcell, The Chinese in
Southeast Asia, 1951: pg. 11)

There can be little doubt that the Chinese had been in Java
for a long time. No doubt that in these long settled
communities, Chinese took local wives and established
families. There was in these early Islamic societies a barrier
to the local assimilation of the Chinese. It is apparent that the
Chinese took wives from the lowest social classes, or slaves,
from non-Islamic groups or the Balinese.

The inferior status of these women precluded their capacity
to culturally assimilate the offspring of these marriages "so
decisively in favor of native culture as did Thai wives."
Furthermore, if sons and daughters remained within the
Chinese community, after a few generations, native-Chinese
intermarriage would decline, as the Chinese community
provided its own wives.

We know that the first headmen or Kapitans of the Chinese
in Seventeenth Century Batavia had Balinese wives, but by
the Eighteenth Century their successors were marrying
daughters of other Chinese officers." (Mary F. Somers-
Heidhues, Chinese Minorities in Southeast Asia, pg. 36-7)

Dutch policies legally prohibited intermarriage of the Chinese
(1717) and their assimilation to native status. They were
quartered off in their own colonies, required to wear typically
Chinese dress and were not permitted freedom of movement
outside of these areas except when in service of the Dutch
interests.

Later, in 1854, such Chinese were set into a separate, higher tax category. Later influx of Chinese Totoks, and especially Chinese women, even further discouraged assimilation and acculturation of this group, and even resulted in some degree of resinification into the newer Chinese communities.

It appears that the Peranakan of Java, and perhaps Baba communities of Malacca, became effectively stabilized sometime between the Seventeenth and Nineteenth Centuries, as effectively closed and self-perpetuating communities that had their own cultural orientation.

Coincidental with this period were Imperial Edicts beginning in the early Eighteenth Century and in effect until the early Nineteenth Century that effectively prevented further emigration from Southeastern China and that strongly discouraged the repatriation of those Chinese abroad, under penalty of punishment.

It was then, during this period that the Chinese communities could no longer look back to China with the hope of some day returning to be buried there. This must have provided a strong incentive for these Chinese to reorient themselves to their local context, to effectively break off their ties to the homeland, and to cultivate a sense of a local cultural orientation that involved some measure of indigenous acculturation and assimilation.

Once formed, these separate and isolated Chinese communities, with their Peranakan cultural practices and orientation, remained effectively segregated up until their eventual disintegration and demise under the modern policies of the state regimes promoting new Indonesian and Malay Nationalisms. Modern ethnicity is a phenomenon of the mass markets and bureaucratic encapsulation of the development of modern nation states and their governing apparatuses of integration.

Peranakan

The earliest evidence for Chinese communities in the Straits must be taken to date from Eunuch Cheng Ho's founding of Malacca in 1408. It can be safely assumed that from the time of its founding, Chinese must have had a regular, if not continuous, residence there.

It is likely that the earliest Chinese settlement had more of the character of a transient camp or a small trading colony than of a settled, internally organized community. "From the available Chinese, Malay and Portuguese sources, it seems certain that there was a Chinese trading community in the port-city of Malacca before the fall of the Sultanate in 1511.

But whether these Chinese represented a permanent or a fluid society, that kept coming and going with the monsoons, is still uncertain. The size of the Chinese trading community was probably small and demographically if not economically insignificant. However, it laid the foundation for the development of a permanent Chinese community in Malacca." (Yeh Hua Fen, Historical Guide of Malacca, 1936)

There is not uniform agreement on this score of the early Chinese settlement of Malacca. Victor Purcell is somewhat skeptical stating that permanent Chinese communities were not established of any significant size until the coming of the Europeans.

It is apparent that Chinese had formed settlements in some of the port cities of Java prior to the European contact, and these perhaps constituted some of the earliest Chinese settlements in the Straits. Mention in the early Portuguese references is only of Chinese junks whose crew and traders remained on board.

A "Campon China" is given on the map in Eredia's history of Malacca, 1613, but this settlement is only of a very small size. The paucity of reference to the Chinese in the early

Portuguese texts on Malacca may not be an indication of the lack of Chinese inhabitants there so much as an indication of the lack of Portuguese attention or interest in such details.

There is a story of Sultan *Mansur Shah*, from 1462, to whom the Emperor of China's daughter, *Hong Li-po*, was sent for their hands in marriage. The Emperor sent a fleet of one hundred "*pilus*" bearing 500 daughters of his *paramantris* as handmaidens to the Princess.

The well mentioned in this reference has long been the source of drinking water famous for its taste, and perhaps its curative properties as well, so much so that its waters have been transported to neighboring countries, as far as Sumatra, during times of drought and pestilence.

The location of the later Bukit China (hill or local prominence), of the Princess *Hung Li-po's* dwelling, on this hill, and the digging of a well at its base, may have been, from the standpoint of Chinese Geomancy, a propitious arrangement.

It seems likely that, sometime between *Cheng Ho's* first visit, in 1403, *Alfonso d' Albuquerque's* conquest of Malacca in 1511, and the Dutch conquest in 1641, Chinese sojournership in early Straits Settlements at some point crossed the thin line (or continuum) to colonial settlement.

Evidence of grave inscriptions at the Chinese cemetery, <u>Bukit Cina</u>, the oldest of which date to the sixteenth century, and the next set which date to the beginning of the Ching Dynasty in the 1644, have some bearing on the early Malacca Chinese. "One of them is that of the husband and wife of a certain Ng by surname...The tombstone of the right one shows that the dead was a Kapitan, surnamed Tay, while that of the left, the Kapitan Nya, or Lady Kapitan or the

Peranakan

Kapitan's wife, probably a native woman...." (Yeh Hua Fen, <u>Historical Guide of Malacca</u>, 1936: pg. 79)

The oldest family lineages of Malacca Chinese, the Tans, Tays and Li traditions, do not go back further than the first half of the seventeenth century. (Victor Purcell, "Chinese Settlement in Malacca. <u>Journal of the Malayan Branch of the Royal Asiatic Society</u>, Vol. XX, Part I, pg. 122-3)

The Dutch give reference to a Chinese community — "The 300 or 400 Chinese shopkeepers, craftsmen and farmers could be allowed to settle down at their own convenience, provided they cultivate the gardens within their territory."

> "They can hire or occupy those empty houses which can be saved from collapse or destruction...The ruined gardens between the river *Boekit Tjina* and the southern suburbs should be lent to Netherlanders, Portuguese, Malaccans, and Chinese to be cultivated...For these some 800 to 1,000 Chinese settlers would be very useful." (Justus Schouten, "Report of 1641 to the Dutch East India Company")

The Dutch appointed "Kapitans China" to manage the Chinese community of Malacca, much as they did in Java and Batavia. "The Chinese living at *Basar* on the north of the city have their own Captain *Notchin* who lives on small merchandise." Thus we get the beginning of a succession of "at least" eleven Kapitans China. These were Hokkiens, and their descendants, who had fled the Manchus and who maintained strong (in) loyalty to the old Ming Dynasty.

By 1678, Governor *Balthasar Bort* gave a census figure of 892 Chinese in Malacca out of a total of 4,884 people. "The Chinese had 81 brick and 51 atap houses with 127 men, 140 women, 159 children, 93 male slaves, 137 female slaves, and 60 children of slaves inside the city limit." (Victor Purcell, 1947: pg. 124)

By 1750 the Chinese population was 2,161, dropping to 1,390 in 1760, which remained stable until the British occupation in 1795.

Most of the Hokkien of this early period were merchants, but this community became joined by a large Hakka contingent of farmers who pioneered into the hinterlands and played an important role in the opening of the interior states. "The famous pioneer of Kuala Lumpur, *Yap Ah Loi*, a *Fui-Chiu* Hakka, was one of them..." (Yeh Hua Fen, <u>Historical Guide of Malacca</u>, 1936: pg. 83)

With the onset of British rule in the Straits Settlements, the Chinese population increased greatly there. The British found the Chinese useful, and did not discourage the Chinese from developing the coolie system, or the "credit-ticket" or "*Kheh-tau*" system, of immigrating indentured Chinese laborers in massive numbers.

Within seven years of the British acquisition of Penang in 1786 and the founding of its fort there in their effort against the French, the Chinese population had increased to over three thousand souls.

Sir Francis Light, the British Founder of Penang, encouraged the Chinese to immigrate there, "whom he held to be 'the only people of the East from whom a revenue may be raised without expense or extraordinary efforts of government.'" (T. Braddel, "Notices of Penang", <u>Journal of the Indian Archipelago</u>, 1850: pg. 641)

The first Chinese to establish themselves in Penang came from a Chinese community in Kedah, and the first Kapitan China was a baba from there named *Koh Lay Huan*. He settled there as a merchant, planter and tax farmer, and maintained one family in Kedah and another in Penang.

His son by his Penang wife accompanied Sir Stanford Raffles to Singapore in its opening in 1819. The other most influential Chinese families were the *Khoos* and the *Kohs*, who were interrelated by marriage. The *Khoo Kong Si* is an old historical monument to be found in Penang today, and surviving evidence of the patrilineal structure of Hokkien Peranakan Straits society.

My wife's father's family may were descended from this lineage. "In the former days long-settled Chinese families in Kedah and Penang had intermarried with Malays, but with increased immigration from China from the middle of the Nineteenth century, this mixed Chinese-Malay or Baba stock tried to marry pure-blooded Chinese." (Yeh Hua Fen, <u>Historical Guide of Malacca</u>, 1936, "An Immigrant Society," pg. 10-11)

It seems apparent that some of the first Chinese there were also the Baba businessmen from Malacca, who rapidly took advantage of the opportunities that were the result of British colonization.

A similar pattern began in Singapore with its founding in 1819, at which time there were no Chinese present, but the Chinese population of which grew to several thousand within a year. "Many of the principal Chinese families of Malacca took part in the opening up and growth of Singapore and Penang, but continued to keep their families and the family houses in Malacca..." (Yeh Hua Fen, <u>Historical Guide of Malacca,</u> 1936, pg. 16)

Thereafter, the Chinese population in the Straits Settlements grew steadily. "In 1840, 5,063 of them arrived, and by 1865, twenty-five years later, the number had increased threefold to

17,439. However, the formation of large and more permanent Chinese communities in Malaya did not take place until the 1880s when large-scale Chinese immigration began.

The influx of Chinese immigrants by the thousands was mainly the result of the establishment of British political control over the Malay states after 1874. The economic development and the law and order brought about by the British served as a great stimulus to immigration, and hence the Chinese population in Singapore and Malaya increased substantially." (Yen Ching-Hwang; The Overseas Chinese and the 1911 Revolution, pg. 4)

A census figure for the Chinese of Singapore in 1848 lists 1,000 "Malacca Chinese" versus 9,000 Hokkiens, 19,000 Tiuchius, 6,000 Cantonese, 4,000 Hakkas and 700 Hainanese. (Seah Eu Chin, "The Chinese in Singapore", Journal of the Indian Archipelago, Vo. 11, 1848:pg. 290)

An 1881 census recorded in Singapore 4,513 "Straits-born" men out of a total Chinese male population of 72,571, and 5,014 "Straits-born" women of a total of 14,195 Chinese females.

It is apparent that during this early era of British colonization, the Baba Chinese held an exclusive advantage over the new "*Singkeh*" Chinese. Maurice Freedman writes that "When Singapore was founded as a British settlement in 1819 Babas were among its first inhabitants, and they occupied throughout the nineteenth century a prominent position in local Chinese society, maintaining leadership within it by virtue of their commercial success and by absorbing ambitious immigrants from China into their ranks." (Freedman, Maurice, "Chinese Kinship and Marriage in Singapore" in The Journal of Southeast Asian History, Volume 3, Issue 2: September, 1962: pg. 65-73)

Peranakan

It is apparent that these Babas also held a kind of monopoly over the institution of marriage among the Chinese of the Straits. "The Chinese who congregate here are a mixed mass from all parts: the unmarried ones among them are very numerous and the married ones very few...upon a general calculation I should suppose there were about 2000 married Chinese." (Seah Eu Chin, "The Chinese in Singapore" <u>Journal of the Indian Archipelago</u>, 1848: pg. 284)

The same author notes that the greatest number of married Chinese men is "found among the Malacca born Chinese; next to them among the Hok-kien shop keepers, then the Tio-Chin.... As for common laborers and coolies and those who have no fixed employment very few among them get married." (Seah Eu Chin, "The Chinese in Singapore" <u>Journal of the Indian Archipelago</u>, 1848: pg. 284)

It was apparent that the local orientation and settled state of the Baba communities in the Straits resulted in the need to establish and maintain a local system of marriage and kinship. With increasing immigration of Chinese into the Straits Settlements, this community soon became a minority of about 10 percent of the Chinese population in Singapore. Most of the Chinese born in the Straits Settlements during this era were Baba by birth.

Before the turn of the Twentieth century, very few Chinese women immigrated into the Straits, and the ratio of men to women in these communities was very imbalanced. "Originally the inhabitants of Malacca, the Babas later spread to the Malay States and other British settlements. With increased immigration, half-caste Sino-Malay girls married immigrants from China as their fathers were reluctant to marry them to Malays, and their <u>progeny</u> would have less Malay and more Chinese blood. In time mixed parentage almost disappeared, but the descendants of the Sino-Malays continued to be known as Babas. Then by the time the

Straits Settlements came into being in 1826 there were few Babas who were actually Sino-Malays." (Png Poh-Seng, 1969: pg. 96-7)

With the turning of the 20th Century, the Straits Settlements were well established within a Nanyang network that extended across the Straits to include the Peranakan communities of Java, as well as hinterland communities in the interior states of Malaya, as well as communities in Borneo, and in Sumatra.

Penang, Malacca and Singapore had all developed into Baba communities along divergent lines—those of Penang being more Chinese, the Malacca more traditionally Sino-Malay, and the Singaporeans, more strongly oriented towards the English due to the role of English in education, modernization, urbanization and development.

The Twentieth century brought with it a basic change in the status and position of the Baba and Peranakan communities of the Straits. Modernization, the importation of Western-styled nationalisms in the form of new political parties and movements, both in China, in many Southeast Asian nations, as well as across the Nanyang, tended to increasingly exclude the participation of the traditionally and colonially oriented Babas.

The Babas had a strongly apolitical economic orientation but lacked the socio-political organization of their Chinese cousins, and their community came into increasing competition with these organizations. This lack of internal organization had its advantages for entrepreneurship and acculturation to the British colonial system, but it had critical disadvantages in the lack of mutual support, political-economic mobilization and organization, etc.

Peranakan

The Babas tended to lack the political conscience which begun to spring up among both the indigenous Malays and the *Singkeh* and "*Totok*" communities—having defined their identity primarily in relation to the British administrative authority. Indeed, in many occasions, their self-professed loyalty to the Queen was more British than the British.

Thus the beginning of the Twentieth Century marked the beginning of the end of the traditional Baba way of life. Baba culture continued to sustain itself as a community, but with increasing adversity and difficulty. It is likely that socially and culturally it became gradually atomized and disintegrated, becoming a kind of home-bound family orientation that had less and less to do with the changing outside world.

They persisted with what became increasingly ethnocentric, snobbish airs of cultural superiority based upon their predecessorial claims, but this was in the face of decreasing relevance and credibility within a modernizing world.

Invasion of Southeast Asia by the Japanese at the outset of World War Two marked the end of Baba supremacy in the Straits Settlements. The Japanese executed many Baba leaders. After the war, the Baba community retained much of its wealth, but lost most of its privilege. Malays in general, as a community, threw in support of the Japanese, and the Japanese empowered the Malays with political power and paramilitary authority in Malaya.

In Singapore, the Babas were effectively absorbed by the larger Chinese component, and "The result of these processes was to make the Singapore Babas less easily distinguishable—especially from the English-educated Chinese; who not only abound but are on the increase." (Clammer, pg. 8)

In Malaysia, the Straits Chinese developed their own political associations, later known as the "Peranakan Association," from about 1900. In Indonesia, the Peranakan were relatively late in forming their own political organizations, remaining politically disinterested and neutral as long as possible, until increasing discrimination encouraged the formation of "*Baperki*" in the late 1950s.

In Penang, Straits Chinese leaders began the Penang Secession movement which lasted from 1948-1951, and which was defeated by the joint efforts of the British and Malay parties. The failure of this movement sealed the fate of the Penang Straits Chinese to determine their own political, economic and social future in relation to the newly emerging nation of Malaysia.

Since the independence period of Malaysia and Indonesia, the Babas and Peranakan have been considered a dying breed and a cultural anachronism of a bygone colonial era. Peranakan status in Indonesia, subsequent to the riots and political upheavals and anti-communist reaction of 1963 and 1965-6, has declined as a segregated community, and the Peranakan seem to have undergone systematic ethnocultural assimilation and loss.

In post-independence Singapore, the Peranakan community was resinified and became increasingly modernized and westernized. Singapore national culture effectively absorbed its Baba basis, using its seemingly western orientation as a basic cultural model for its modernization—in the process Baba culture in Singapore has become a thing of the past without much relevance to a nation preoccupied with modern development.

Old Chinese sections of the city, a nostalgic reminder of the Chinese colonial past, have nearly been completely razed to make room for modern business buildings, malls and tenement flats.

In modernizing Malaysia, the Chinese community in general, including the Babas, has been on one hand effectively segregated through structural and social discrimination, and has on the other hand endured under systematic policies designed to encourage communal segregation and enforce cultural assimilation to the Malay national culture that remains traditionally fundamentalist Muslim in orientation.

The Babas of Malacca have been more or less symbolically appropriated as an anachronistic model of Sino-Malay cultural assimilation. The Babas of Penang and elsewhere have seen their community basically split apart—some becoming reabsorbed by Hokkien and *Tieu Chiu* Chinese communities, others more inclined to the English language and British culture, being left furthest out on the limb, with many who could afford the cost migrating to the Common Wealth countries.

Ethnic revitalization can only happen in a dominant society that honors its cultural heritage and traditions—and yet this can prove to be almost as ethno-historically revisionist as a society that seeks to hide or erase its past.

Past cultural forms and models can be adopted by an emerging middle and upper-middle class, which is defined by its standardized national cultural orientation, as almost a kind of national mythology and as a form of elaborate play which mediates the new and old in the transformations of the past into the present. The past becomes a sounding board for both justice and injustice in the present.

As an intermediate, somewhat transitional cultural model, Sino-Malay Baba culture can and has been appropriated by both Singaporean and Malay societies to legitimate a larger range of national cultural interests—different elements of the original culture have been highlighted and emphasized, and other, contradictory aspects, conveniently ignored or even forgotten:

"The Baba is thus faced with a terribly difficult identity problem…Multiracialism as a policy may well therefore have the (presumably unintended) consequence of artificially supporting minority cultures which in the normal course of events would probably pass naturally away." (John Clammer; 1980: 139)

Yet the contradiction was not a part of the original culture, but a part of the current conflict of competing identities, interests and trajectories.

III: Nonya Culture

An old theory of cultural dynamics (Melville Herskovits, 1948) maintains that any culture has a central focus within which it highly develops certain attributes, the elaboration and variation of which leads to a directional development of the culture along certain distinctive pathways—a culture drifts and moves in these directions. The socialization of children combines with the sanctioning of habituated, acquired adult behavior, to perpetuate a cultural pattern and its transmission through time.

Possibilities of deviation and alteration exist in the socialization process, in adults who willingly go against the sanctioned norms, and in the process of cultural elaboration itself. This theoretical orientation is important in understanding the culture of the Babas and Nonyas, as a certain complex of cultural Peranakan attributes was highly elaborated, and that provided a sense of center and focus for its cultural orientation.

It has been argued that the Babas did not in fact possess their own culture—rather, they possessed a distinctive ethnicity that became translated in certain specific ways.

> "... The term "Baba Chinese" is commonly used as an ethnic label and it should not be assumed that since there is such a thing as an ethnic group there must therefore be a Baba Chinese culture which is shared by all Baba Chinese and entirely distinct from other ethnic groups.... (Cecilia Ng Siew Hua, 1983: pg. 98-9)

Such an argument begs the critical question of where we should draw the line between an ethnic group and a genuine culture, and how we should define either culture or ethnicity in contrast to one another.

In this regard, the Babas had shared with the rest of the Nanyang, albeit not as strongly, in the basic Chinese organizational principles, an ethos of ethnos—such that ethnic identity and difference became the basis of a shared cultural orientation.

It seems that socio-cultural barriers of language, religion, custom and belief were great enough to have caused an effective separation, isolation and emergent distinctiveness of cultural orientation among the Babas and Peranakan.

Barriers to marriage and mobility by Chinese in Islamic society, unless proclaiming faith in Islam and forgoing one's own, usually cherished, Chinese cultural identity, were strong enough to prevent rapid or complete assimilation of the Chinese merchant communities.

These communities also maintained some modicum of contact with the Chinese mainland and with other Chinese communities, as well as with a broader, outside world. These Chinese had an Imperial civilization several thousand years old to look back to as a source of ethnic pride, identity and solace—a civilization that was quite developed and sophisticated for its time.

Chinese have long been notoriously Sino-centric in their value orientation and world-view, wherever they may be found. They never give up completely a core of Chinese-ness. Furthermore, these communities were likely to have received periodic injections of new immigrants, sojourners, or refugees who were navigating the Nanyang, even during its era of Imperial ostracism and isolation from China.

Thus, community separateness of these early Chinese in Java and Malacca was defined as much from without as from within. Once these communities had grown to a sufficient size, say several thousand, they became stable enough to be both racially and culturally self-perpetuating.

The two or three hundred year period of their early pre-modern development was certainly long enough for the emergence of a unique cultural orientation to be well-formed and virtually complete in most aspects.

In this regard we only have to look back upon our own shallow sense of American history to see how quickly, and firmly, a typically "American" character and culture formed in the world, and what its consequences may have been in the world.

It is possible that the base of this cultural orientation developed relatively early in its basic form, and once having come into being, grew in size and elaborateness, but remained basically the same to be perpetuated via "ethno-endogamy" (community closure) through the many generations. This pattern is not uncommon among many other minority communities vis-à-vis host societies around the world.

It is difficult to refute, or interpret, the material evidence for Baba culture. Silver-work, Chinaware, styles of dress, cuisine, marriage customs, speech, all suggest a basic difference and shared uniqueness of the Babas from either more traditionally oriented Chinese on the one hand, and the locally predominant Muslim Malay culture on the other.

To attempt to triangulate Baba ethno-culture, we can sense a convergence of the evidence toward support for the idea of a distinctive cultural orientation. Distinctive aspects of Baba culture emerge in language, religion, material culture, social structure and organization, in values, world-view, in literature, as well as in self-professed aspects of personal identity and group affiliation.

Furthermore, if the Babas and their Peranakan cousins in Java in fact constituted a unique cultural grouping in the world, then there is a need to find some sense of focus and center for such an orientation, as well perhaps as a sense of its own self-styled "raison d'etre" and basic understanding in relation to the world.

The most unique and defining cultural characteristic of the closed cultural focus of Baba and Peranakan culture was upon the domestic life of its womenfolk. Virtually every material artifact that is identified as distinctively Baba is related to the personal dress, adornment, cooking, and marriage of the women. It is something of a paradox that we should choose to call it "Baba" culture as opposed to "Nonya" culture.

This focus fit the historical picture of the origin of the culture- women had central domestic value and marriage- reproductive status, as they were relatively few in an immigrant colony context that was heavily male-biased.

John Clammer speaks of the "rarity-value" of girls in such a society, which accounts for the seclusion imposed upon younger women, especially unmarried Nonyas, as well as for the relatively high status of Nonyas, and even for the frequent occurrence of female heads of households.

> "A woman, particularly an elderly one, would on the death of her husband become household head, rather than allowing such a position to fall to her eldest son. This is not so surprising when one recognizes that she would already have been exercising considerable (if informal) social power in her household." (Clammer, 1980:38)

Pernakan

It seems likely that the Nonya wives of the Chinese were the
principle elaborators of its distinctive cultural traits. They
were not the silver smiths, potters and craftsmen who made
and elaborately decorated these artifacts, but they may have
been the mothers-in-law of the craftsmen, as well as the
principle buyers of the wares.

It also seemed as if the cultural orientation was set up, from
early on, to secure its reproductive base, to confer upon its
women a special, privileged status which made them
symbolically and socially attractive in lucrative marriage
arrangements, and to promote a social structure that was
based upon "marrying in" to the community rather than
marrying out, and to "marry up" the social ladder rather than
across or down.

> "In addition to such voluntary unions, it was possible for
> the Baba community to purchase Malay girls who were
> debt slaves or to marry those who were partial outcasts
> because of their social behavior." (L.A.P. Gosling, 1964:
> 216)

If the original wives of the original Babas were in fact of low
status or they were slaves or concubines, then these wives
must have from early on formed their own sense of anti-
structural communitas, within the context of which they
elaborated their own symbolic system that they subsequently
bequeathed to their children and grandchildren.

This female orientation of Baba culture would explain the
relatively a-political nature of its orientation, and the freedom
that the Baba male had in defining his own identity as either
Chinese "*Towkay*," vis-à-vis Western "*Orang Pute*."

The male was involved almost exclusively in mercantile
activities that accrued material wealth to the household and
the community.

If perchance he became a leader, a "Kapitan China," or a Towkay, then this was done so on a model that was more appropriately, prototypically Nanyang Chinese. It is noteworthy in this regard that the Babas wore either western dress or Chinese costume, but rarely the Malay sarong. On the other hand, the customary dress for the Nonya was the Malay sarong and kerbaya, adorned with jewelry distinctively Peranakan in style. The Baba was quick and emphatic in stressing his Chinese identity—the Nonya was persistent in cultivating a more domestic Malay style of life.

If this was the case, then the apolitical character of Baba culture allowed the male the freedom and capacity to acculturate and accommodate different political symbol systems—either Western or Chinese or Malay, without his cultural identity as "Baba" being threatened or compromised.

"Money making", prowess in money handling, and the pursuit of economic opportunities took precedence over political networking and opportunity seeking or over having power to control other people or communities.

It was not that the Baba could not deal politically in life. Indeed, he often did so with unusual talent—rather his cultural orientation allowed him the freedom to engage politically or not without cultural constraint. Notions of territoriality and boundary were negotiable. About the only real political boundary firmly in place being that boundary which secured the domestic life of the Nonya centric culture.

The domestic life of the Nonya women, perhaps being more religiously oriented rather than political, constituted the core of the Baba culture. It is noteworthy in this regard that the Nonya women were rarely themselves engaged in petty trade—a not uncommon preoccupation among Southeast Asian women in general. Rather, they were engaged in domestic management, and perhaps as well, in their husband's bookkeeping.

Furthermore, they were renowned as inveterate gamblers, with their own style of card game. It can be expected that the religious patterns of the Nonyas were distinctive in several ways that helped to reinforce and reflect this somewhat exaggerated domesticity and female orientation of the culture.

Nonya women had eventually achieved, within their cultural universe, a degree of independence, autonomy and status that was not characteristic of their more traditional Chinese or Malay sisters. "A change came over our people. With good intentions, certain people relaxed the old rules and gradually the old restrictions became impossible, and almost all at once our Nonyas insisted on their <u>rights</u>.... All the evils complained of against the Nonyas may be traced to the pernicious bondage under which they have been brought up...." ("Our Nonyas" <u>Straits Chinese Magazine</u>; Vol. VII, No. 4, Dec. 1904) They were not marked off as an inferior caste, but came to claim for themselves the principle prerogatives of their culture.

Uxorilocal residence (living at the bride's home) patterns have long remained a curiously anomalous feature of Baba culture—institutional arrangements that have persisted historically in spite of the loss of its original cause and reason. The wife's spouse married into and lived in the mother's household. The senior Nonya in such a situation would come to have a degree of influence, especially when her husband was away on business that would make their status and position in society enviable.

The wife would retain a measure of respect and familial support she would not have if she had moved into the husband's parent's household. The husband would find himself in a peculiar position, especially for a more traditional male not brought up in such a household, in which he would have to compromise some of his male prerogatives, and in which he would find himself compelled to achieve in ways he may not otherwise have done.

The male, and the son, probably retained much of his privileged, paternal Chinese status. But he was more compelled to define that identity exclusively in terms that was outside the household, and, furthermore, basically outside of the central bounds of the culture of which he was attached, if not by birth, then by marriage. His only cultural obligation was to protect and support his domestic base of support, but not necessarily to dominate it or to be a central part of its domestic orientation.

According to my wife who is a direct descendant of Nonyas, the father would take out the male child into the outside world, while the female child would remain in the domestic world of the mother.

The following is a summary of most of the cultural traits that are identified as distinctly Baba and Nonya. It is worth reiterating that these traits are all related to the world of the Nonya.

Straits Silverwork

A long tradition of local handiwork by Chinese silversmiths dating back to at least the Sixteenth or Seventeenth Century, and which became obsolete in the early 20th Century, produced many kinds of objects now quite rare that belonged to a distinctive style and tradition. Silver and silver-gilt articles were long regarded by Nonyas as status symbols (Ho Wing Meng, 1976: 38)

Pernakan

They commissioned or bought from local silversmiths mostly fine items of jewelry for personal adornment, ornamental articles and "utensils specifically to give that added touch of luxury and ostentation to their ornately furnished homes." (Ho Wing Meng, 1976: pg. 38)

These articles were not the large size of similar European goods, but were confined to "personal ornaments, objects of virtue, occasional pieces of trophies, decorative bowls with matching saucers and spoons, little tea-cups, teapots, wine-ewers, pillow and bolster plates, incense burners, curtain hooks, ornamental plaques, little vases and betel nut or sireh boxes." (Ho Wing Meng, 1976, pg. 38)

Extant pieces of antique Straits silverwork are generally small, fine, and noted for their intricate workmanship. Their decorative motifs first present to the eye a chaotic confusion lacking unity of theme. Phoenixes, Dragons, Lions, dogs, are set against a floral background of *prunus* blossoms, chrysanthemums, lotuses and peonies, occasionally interspersed by Buddhist-Taoist symbols.

This heterogeneous assortment of motifs made such silverwork unappealing to early connoisseurs as compared to the more elegant and simple designs of Malay silverwork that presented only geometric or arabesque floral motifs.

The bulk of this silverwork was intended as wedding gifts, and the symbolisms portrayed carried Chinese cultural-religious significance for the recipient of the gift. The style, though cluttered and thematically un-unified, is exuberant with energy and is so clean and clear in relief that it often conveys a sense of three-dimensionality.

Thus the Chinese silversmith differed from his Malay counterpart not only by giving more attention to the symbolic significance of the art motifs he employed, but he was rarely constrained by his religion or social conventions from expressing his artistic inspirations in terms of a very restricted category of art symbols.

Indeed, if he so desired, he was at liberty to draw from his pantheistic and hospitable system of religious beliefs and folklores, an enormous and varied repertoire of motifs, both conventional and symbolic, that, among other things, included at least a dozen of botanical species of flowering plants and fruit trees, shells, crustaceans and mammals.

If these proved to be inadequate, there was a generous supply of extraordinary beasts and beings culled from mythologies going back to time immemorial, to enrich his decorative themes. (Ibid, pg. 42-3)

Not all Straits silver was this fussy. Some is of quite simple design, and some is done with an eye for patterned symmetry.

Overall, the conception of design of Straits silver is held to be simple and recognizably clear—for its ornateness and intricacy its patterns are rarely distorted or ornamentally overburdened. Chinese silversmiths preserved the original form and integrity of the basic utensil no matter what the design—the ornate and varied designs are exclusively relief as opposed to chased or engraved works.

Buntal pillow plates for embellishing bridal pillows were adopted from ancient Hindu-Javanese civilization of Palembang and Kedah.

Other kinds of articles included bracelets, Nonya hairpins, sireh boxes, curtain hooks, ornamental bells, caskets or "*ganchu ranjang*", and talismans for the bridal bed, distinctive belts and buckles worn by Nonyas, ladies purses, key holders, brooches, "*kerosangs*" or buttons for the front of the *kerbaya* blouses, necklaces and chains, earrings, finger rings, anklets, hairpins ("*kerok kuping chuckuk sanggul*"

Pernakan

which means to "scratch the ear, pierce through the hair"), as well as other miscellaneous items such as chopsticks, pocket plaques, buttons, "and other types of ornamental accessories for the bridal trousseau." (Png Poh-Seng, 1969: pg. 89-95)

".... The majority of Straits Silverworks...may generally be dated back to the nineteenth century; for it was during this period that the baba community reached its zenith of prosperity; so that large quantities of silver ornaments, jewelry and other objects of virtue were turned out to meet the requirements of the Nonyas whose love of ostentatious display was proverbial.... By the 'twenties or the 'thirties Straits silverworks had virtually become a thing of the past." (Png Poh-Seng, 1969: pg. 95)

Nonya Ware

The Nonya's were renowned for the elaborate and richly decorated porcelain—noted for their rich colors and elaborate designs"...In the days gone by, the wealthier babas spared no expenses or trouble to procure direct from the famous porcelain-centre of *Ching-te'-chen*, Kiangsi Province, grandiloquent vases, ornamental jars, gold-fish bowls, flower pots with matching stands, ceremonial basins and complete dinner services and tea sets sometimes running into thousands of pieces specially designed and decorated to their own specifications." (Ho Wing Meng, 1976: pg. 38)

The designs of these pieces are noted for their multiple colors, their variety and richness of design, and for the presence of design patterns on the inside of bowls and plates.

My wife's mother owned a collection of this dinner-ware handed down from her grandmother, which my wife would have inherited were they not destroyed in the container in which they had been packed away. According to my wife, they consisted of plates and bowls of various sizes, spoons, and a big porcelain soup ladle. The designs were deep, muted blue in color, of an indistinct wavy floral pattern — brushed on designs that were undefined.

Nonya Costume

The "*baju panjang*," a long sleeved, knee length, thin transparent blouse, with scalloped edges, worn with an inner white undershirt, held together by the "*kerosangs*," a set of "three round silver-gilt or gold brooches studded with pearls and other precious stones." Underneath a sarong was worn.

Nonyas tied their hair into a top bun, tied with three pins. For special occasions, cloth slippers are worn, "often richly embroidered with silk or gold threads, sequins, beads and gilded ornaments." (Png Poh-Seng, 1969: 110)

"Except for young girls, a large handkerchief folded diagonally into a triangular shape was usually draped over the right shoulder as part of their outfit. This was fastened to the <u>baju</u> with a jewel brooch from which might dangle a bunch of gold lucky charms." (Png Poh-Seng, 1969: pg.110)

The style of Nonya dress has seemed to change over the generations. From about the "*baju panjang*" gave way to the sarong and kerbaya, introduced by the Javanese Peranakan and adapted from the Malay "*baju kurong*" similar to the "*baju panjang*" worn by elderly Nonyas.

The Kerbaya was adopted by younger Nonyas, a shorter version of the "*baju panjang*" made of muslin-like or voile fabric and much more elegant in appearance. The Nonyas used a great deal of fine floral or foliage lace in their kerbayas, the best embroidery coming from Javanese Chinese tailors. This was worn over an inner vest-coat.

Pernakan

The Nonya kerbaya differs somewhat from the Malay or Indonesian forms by being looser fitting, whereas the latter are typically body hugging "V" shaped "tapering towards the waist and then flaring downwards to emphasize the women's narrow waist-lines." (Ho Wing Meng, 1976: pg. 27) The tighter fitting form has been adopted by the younger Nonyas—the grandchildren of the Nonyas of a half-century ago who wore the more traditional "*baju panjang*."

The Nonyas adopted their own style of hair-dressing from the Indonesian and Malay customs of combing their hair backwards in long tresses which are twisted and turned into a large loose knot, shaped like a donut, at the back of the head, which is secured by clips and pins.

The Nonyas combed their hair very tightly back in the form of a long plait held together by the application of water glue, and twisted into a small, tight topknot called "*sanggul siput*," which means literally "sea shell."

Through the topknot would be inserted three long hairpins of about 7 inches length. The first pin was inserted directly through the hair knot. The second pin, more delicate and decorative with a splay of leaves set with pearls or stones, was inserted crossways at from the first pin at the base of the hair bun. "The third and smallest hairpin, similarly designed, is inserted into the stem of the knot."(Ho Ming Weng, 1976: 27-8)

> Like their Malay and Indonesian counterparts, the Nonyas sometimes inserted jasmines and other highly scented flowers into their hair buns." (Ho Ming Weng, 1976:27-8)

Among the wealthier Babas, it was customary for the Nonyas to wear gold or silver-gilt belts elaborately designed to form either a complex band of little interlocking rings superimposed with granule works of florets, or a parallel series of thickly pleated strands held in position at regular intervals by ornamental clips.

These belts are always secured together by impressive buckles or clasps, most of which are decorated with chased and repouse works of complex design. Such belts were primarily intended to secure the sarong firmly around the waist, but they also served as objects of personal adornment.

The Nonyas also hanged a bunch of keys from an ornamental key-holder clipped on to belt on one side of the girth, and a silver hanging purse, usually made of fine wire-work or a network of tiny interlocking rings and superimposed with granule' works, from the other side of the belt.

As for the kerbaya that comes embroidered with birds and floral motifs in front and along the side edges, the frontal hems are secured together not by buttons but with a set of three _kerosang_; or brooches joined together by delicate tassels.

Each of these is fashioned after the form of a floral spray set with diamonds, pearls, rubies or other precious and semi-precious stones in _jour settings_. The older type of _kerosangs_ however, is of much simpler design; it consists of three circular rings mounted with pearls or stones, or two circular rings and a heart-shape broach. These brooches are never connected together by tassels. (Ibid, pg.28)

Nyonya women were noteworthy for their over-dressing and ornamental ostentation of jewelry. "It has been suggested that many wives pestered their husbands to buy them valuable jewels to enhance their security; others found in diamonds a salve for the trials and tribulations of domestic life" (Png Poh-Seng, 1969:111)

> "When a Straits Chinese lady attended a luncheon party, she preened herself like a peacock would its feathers, radiant with sparkling jewels, thus showing off her fortunate circumstances and size of her husband's fortune. On that

Pernakan

> day it was a matter of blatant advertisement to all and sundry of one's husband's financial circumstances. In fact many a husband had been blackmailed into buying jewels for his spouse on grounds that her being bedecked with jewels would reflect his prosperity." (Rosie Tan Kim Neo, "The Straits Chinese in Singapore, A Study of the Straits Chinese Way of Life", Unpublished Research Paper, University of Malaya, Singapore, 1958; pg. 102)

Nonya Beadwork and Embroidery

Nonyas made in their homes colorful beadwork and embroidery for which they became well known. They embroidered their kerbayas in colorful, lacy flora and animal patterns. They also made in their homes very fine and delicate beaded "bumboat shoes."

They made cloth shoes, slippers, vases, purses, spectacle holders, jewelry containers, and wedding-ornaments out of colorful beads—items that resemble in both design and form both the silverwork and the ceramics.

Mothers taught their daughters and the work was mostly domestic. They used tiny beads and special threads of silver and gold. Designs incorporated animals from the Chinese Lunar Calendar as well as floral motifs.

Nonya Cuisine

Nonya cuisine is spicy, using a lot of tamarind, coconut milk, chili, banana leaves for wrapping and *balachan*, a fermented shrimp paste, "*petai*" and "*jering*", a kind of seed, "*gulai*" curry, and *Kueh*, small cakes using a lot of coconut milk, *gula malacca*, or brown sugar, screw-pine leaf, or "*daun-pandan*," "*bunga telang*," giving the *Kueh* coloring, wrapped in banana leaves and steamed.

Chinese dishes would be added variations of fragrant seasonings to give an extra tang to the dishes—"Food which is neither hot nor spicy is considered unsavory to Peranakan palate." Nonya cuisine has largely passed away, except for a revived interest and taste in it as an "ethnic food."

Among the Hainanese of Singapore, Nonya food became a part of their own style of cooking. "Until recently the Hainanese cake-vendor popularly known as the *'Otah'* man was a familiar sight in Singapore. His daily visit was welcomed by most Straits Chinese women and children." (Png Poh-Seng, footnote, pg. 100)

While residing several months in Penang, our street would be visited daily by an Indian man on a bicycle peddling Nonya "*kueh*," sweet cakes and curry puffs.

My wife always delighted in his coming, and thereby first introduced me to the blue-green sweet rice cakes of the Nonyas.

"The preparation of food in Nonya style, it should be noted in passing, is a complex and laborious process, and it may be for this reason too, that this sophisticated art might be irretrievably lost when the last surviving generation of elderly Nonyas passes from the scene." (Ho Wing Meng, 1976: 30)

Nonya cuisine is said to have been similar to that of the Peranakan of Java. According to the ethnography of the <u>Peranakan of Sukabumi</u> by Tan Giok-Lan, the Peranakan preferred food basically Javanese in style—dry boiled rice, sate, goat, chicken, beef, pork, vegetables, especially "*pete*" and "*djengko*", a *sourish* vegetable soup called "*sajur assem*," a kind of salad called "*gado-gado*" served with fried bean curd or "*tempe*" and peanut-cake or "*ontjom*."

Pernakan

My wife on occasion has made for me "*gado-gado*," served with "krupuk" or fried shrimp chips. "The popularity of this dish is indicated by the fact that it appears at the table of even the elaborate parties of wealthy Peranakan." (Tan Giok-Lan, 1963:42-5)

Chinese elements incorporated into this menu include Chinese noodles, or "*Mie*," or "*Hokkien Mi*" or "*mee*," bean-curd, "*tao hu*" or "*tahu*," bean sprouts, or "*taoge*," bean sauce, or "*taotjio*," soya sauce called "*ketjap,*" and dried shrimp called "*hebi.*"

All these imported items are known by terms derived from Hokkien—an indication of the Hokkien origins of the Peranakan of Java. "As with most of the food of Chinese origin, a Peranakan noodle dish looks and tastes different from a Totok one." (Tan Giok-Lan, 1963: pg. 44)

We might also say that Peranakan have reintegrated the influences they have encountered so that something new has been created, that might very well be called Peranakan food.

We have also noted that in the realm of food we find one of the few clear instances of reverse acculturation, whereby traits of Chinese origin have been incorporated into the Indonesian way of life. (Tan Giok-Lan, 1963, pg. 45)

"To sum up, food among the Peranakan is basically Indonesian in origin with important elements of Chinese origin, plus a few western items. The significant thing is that three elements have in almost all cases been modified from the original, although the origin is still recognizable. It would appear that Western items are most radically modified, Totok Chinese items next, while items of Indonesian origin have been modified the least. (Tan Giok-Lan, 1963: 42-5)

Sireh Chewing, Tea and Cards

The chewing of sireh, or betel nut, is a common Southeast Asian trait adopted by the Nonyas, who are alone among the Nanyang Chinese in practicing this custom. A thin layer of quicklime paste was applied over the sireh leaf, along with a sprinkle of the astringent gambier and thin slices of areca nut. The leave is folded into a small square and then chewed. Chewing the leaf has a slight narcotic effect, is bitter in taste, and stains the mouth a reddish color.

It was customary politeness to offer sireh to guests, and the sireh service; "*tepak sireh*" was a standard accouterment of the Nonya household.

My wife remembers these sireh sets, simple lacquered pieces not as ornate as the fancier silver ones found in the picture books. The set consisted of a small lidless box with four smaller caskets and cups on a tray. "No important social function went by without the presences of that ubiquitous *'tepak sireh*.'" (Ho Wing Meng. 1976: pg. 29)

The exchange of betel nut was an important part of the prenuptial ceremonies of a Nonya wedding. For the most part, Sireh-chewing was mostly a Nonya habit rarely adopted by men.

Sireh-serving was typically accompanied by tea, a typically Chinese and un-Malay aspect of the practice—steeped in fine porcelain teapots and served in small, dainty teacups. The Malays customarily served coffee instead of tea.

My wife remembers that her mother would brew up both coffee and tea for her guests.

Nonya women were noted for the frequency with which they were brought before British courts on charges of gambling.

Pernakan

They played a card game called "*chap-ji-ki*" or "*Cherki*," that required four players. The games would last a long time, several hours running. Nonyas would pay little children to shuffle the deck.

My wife mentions the long narrow cards that they would play with, and their special style of handling these cards. They would gamble with money, or even jewelry.

One court case involved eleven Nonyas, reported by a husband of one of players who had lost $50,000 in jewelry and had attempted to replace this by cheap imitations.

"The other event was known as the '*Wong-tye-sin*' case. *Wong-tye-sin* was a god of fortune that had come into prominence by prescribing medicine during an outbreak of the plague in Canton some fifteen years before. This god had been brought to Singapore and four shrines had been opened, whither a large number of <u>Nonyas</u> went for advice as to lottery tickets..." (Song Ong Siang, 1967: 440-1)

Baba Architecture

Some evidence suggests that in some cases, an architectural variant in interior house design, and in the design of business fronts, existed among the Peranakan— incorporating both Malay, Chinese and European styles and designs.

The interior usually contains a large central hall, for receiving guests and for the location of an ancestral altar. The altar is on the far side, facing the front doors and the steps up to the house. "While the staircase of the house is a cultural feature of the Malays, it is treated as if it were the main entrance of a traditional Chinese house and is built at the position that fits into Chinese architectural thinking." (Tan Chee-Beng, 1982: pg.34-8)

"The individual houses are impressive from the perspective of architecture, and the Chinese themselves are proud of them. They are built in distinct traditional style that shows a mixture of Malay and Chinese architectural patterns. (Ibid, 1982: pg. 34-8)

Constructed of fine hardwood and left unpainted, they have a saddle shaped roof and a large veranda that is often open only on the front and enclosed on three sides. The main entrance to the house itself is in the center of the back of the veranda through a set of double doors that opens into the central hall.

At the back of this hall, directly opposite the entrance, is the household altar. To the sides of the main hall, and sometimes behind it, are the bedrooms.

"On either side of the main doors are small barred and shuttered windows and above the door are a set of square 'eyes' (*mata*). This central part of the house is raised four or five feet above the ground, with a stairway located again at the middle of the veranda, just opposite the main doors..."(Robert Winzeler, 1985: 24-25)

Usually built on stilts, they are raised off the ground, and the spot on which they are built are also raised slightly. These houses vary slightly depending upon the affluence of the families living in them.

But such adherence to traditional building styles is also uncharacteristic of either the Malays or the urban dwelling Chinese. Windows are small and barred, and the interior is dimly lit. Bedrooms lead off to either side of the central hall, flanking it. The kitchen may be located on either side or to the back of the house.

"In general, the rural Peranakan Chinese houses outwardly look Malay-like, yet on closer examination, it is also very Chinese...Not only are certain architectural designs Chinese, as we have seen, the functions of certain parts of the house also manifest traditional Chinese culture. For example, the hall or *thian* is the ritual center of the house not only for placing the altar, but also for placing the coffin

> when an adult member of the family passes away. (Tan, 1987: 38)

> This conforms to traditional Chinese thinking. Thus, we may say that the rural Peranakan Chinese house structure is a material manifestation of Peranakan Chinese culture. Just like studying the Peranakan Chinese house structure, we should not be misled by certain overt cultural features of the Peranakan Chinese (like dress and language) and conclude that these Chinese have been assimilated by the Malays...(Tan, 1987: 38)

My wife drew me a floor plan of her Grandmother's house. The floor plan is remarkably similar to that mentioned above, complete with the central hall, flanking bedrooms, front door and stairway, ancestral altar and kitchen. Like most of these rural homes, it was built up upon stilts, and had an atap and corrugated tin roof.

Nineteenth and early twentieth century architectural design in Singapore and Penang, especially of the shop houses of Chinese businesses, suggest a distinctive "Straits" style that incorporates elements of an English tradition with those of the Chinese.

It was a style sometimes referred to as "Chinese Baroque" or "Chinese Palladian"—"that unique neo-classical European architecture, characterized Greco-Roman columns, and the Peranakan-Chinese style originating in Malacca" (Ilsa Sharp, <u>The Straits Times</u>, April 28,1979.)

The facades of these houses often presented a smallish appearance that belied the multi-floored spaciousness within.

> "The *rumah ahkay ahkay* was simple in structure despite the trimmings of the <u>batu ribbon</u> or 'ribbon stone' found in some of these houses. Brightly-coloured ceramic tiles of floral motifs graced part of the front of the house, next to the windows of the upper floors and the lower parts of the walls which lined the five-foot-ways." (Felix Chia, 1980: 83)

Interiors of wealthy Straits Chinese homes also showed traits typically Baba. "A whole new culture, reflected in quite unique forms, including the domestic interior, had grown out of the amalgam of Chinese, Malay, and European ways. Certainly in their desire to identify with their British overlords, the Straits Chinese were the first to enthusiastically embrace Western fashions internally and externally." (Norman Edwards, 1990: 122-3)

Generally, in Straits Chinese terrace houses, guests were entertained in a front hall containing the principle altar of the household, "dedicated to the Goddess of Mercy, *Kwan Yin*, and the God of Wealth." Set behind the altar was a wall or screen to deflect the path of evil spirits and to demarcate the first hall from the second, immediately behind.

> "Views beyond this screen of the interior of the house—its succession of courts and interior spaces—were only admitted gradually and under privilege. Distant acquaintances and visitors were allowed into the first hall only. Friends and closer colleagues were taken into the second hall. In the truly traditional Peranakan household, close relatives and other members of the family and lifelong friends were granted admission to the third or the fourth halls." (Edwards, 1990: 154)

In these houses, the arrangement of rooms was influenced by the subjugation of women in the family hierarchy, whereas in the Straits Chinese family, for the grandmother, it was rather the other way round.

Unlike the young Nonya granddaughters who were expected to be meek and submissive, in general the elder lady was accorded considerable authority in running the household, that she was expected to manage with a firm hand and in a strict, even fierce, uncompromising manner. Such authority was recognized in the setting aside of part of the house as her territory. More often than not, this took the form of her own lounge-dining-room and sleeping quarters and, as in the case of *Hock Gwee Thian*'s house in Prinsep Street, the provision of her very own reclining arm-chair. (Edwards, 1990: pg. 176)

Pernakan

Peranakan Furniture

Closely related to the architecture was the distinctive design of the furniture that completed the interior—ornately carved, inlaid wooden pieces were common in the homes of the wealthy, and simpler but similar pieces could be found in the more humble homes.

Peranakan furniture include the "*tu kacha*," or glass cupboard; black and white wooden sofas and chairs, or "*hup soo ee*;" a movable screen called the "*kepong angin*" or "blocking of the wind;" a Nonya dressing table, or "*mega sanggol rambot*;" and the reclining armchair, or "*krosi sandah*,"

The shortlist also includes jewelry boxes, and the elaborate, grand "*ranjang kemantin*," or "the bride's bed," complete with overhead curtain screens.

IV: Peranakan People

Ethnoculture exists within an historical stream, a human confluence of social change in the world. It is defined from without in interrelationship with a wider world as much as it is generated and defined from within by the people who compose and continuously reconfigure its patterning. The possibilities for development of this pattern always exist across time and space in a wider field of opportunity and risk.

We search for a so-called base-line called "Nonya culture"—some normative or ideal sense of a conventional, traditional center, and find only a continuous stream of variation upon a few basic themes—themes that are defined as much by the exceptions as by the rule.

We find in Nonya culture the presence of stratified Straits Chinese Society quite oriented around domestic Nonya styles, with evidence of male craft and labor specialization, architecture, furniture, ceramics and silverwork, catering to Nonya tastes and preferences.

We then arrive at the conclusion that such a base-line conceptualization of an ideal cultural orientation possessing some kind of "center" is at best a statistical statement of averages, likelihood, and central tendencies, and at worst someone's reified, factitious fiction—a projection of our own superficial sense of reality.

In searching for the external outlines of Peranakan social reality, there are four sets of variables which appear salient, and which may be upon a more general level of understanding somehow interrelated with one another in rendering the conception of Peranakan social reality significant within a larger world. These four variables include: social patterning, religious orientation, language, and, finally, what has become known as ethnicity.

In a more general sense, the convergence of these four salient aspects of Peranakan culture is upon what has been referred to as the social construction of reality. It is a glimpse into the daily dynamics of the Peranakan world, and how its members interact to produce, individually and collectively, a socially constructed and shared world.

Part of this process has to do with social praxis and performance—with the sense of presentation of self in the everyday world.

Part of it has to do with the process of social production— externalization and objectification of a shared stock of knowledge, symbolisms and values, and part deals with the dialectically complementary process of social reproduction— with the problem of socio-cultural transmission of these externalized forms, and their internalizations, or subjectification, into the individual personality.

These processes can be seen to be "functioning" dialectically at several levels—the infra-structural level of economic adaptation, the social structural level of social interaction and integration, and the super-structural level of ideology—and these three levels themselves constitute a sort of parallel-processing dialectical system, a "complex" self-organizing system with a robust sense of historical structure that involves numerous interacting and mutually limiting variables.

It is important to see that this set of social processes is also occurring and impinging upon a larger stream of social reality. The social construction of human reality is also, concomitantly, the psychological construction of human reality.

Social definition of self and the psychological definition of society are also part of larger processes of human civilization, processes that involve boundary identification, projection, psycho-social reference, accommodation, acculturation, assimilation, etc. Both self and society are defined in mutual interrelation with one another, and with a larger world of otherness that has both psychological and sociological components and outcomes.

Peranakan society, wherever it had taken root and flourished, wherever it had spread its seed, always had its own sense of order, organization, purpose and outlook upon the world. It has always had some kind of class structure within which each member's status-role identity has been shaped and measured.

It has long had its hopes for the future espoused in its own way of bringing up its youngest generation, and a sense of present importance with the generation that has come of age in the world, and an orientation toward the past that is passing away with the oldest.

If we look closely, we find that Peranakan society has always been composed of a seamless web of people caught up in the trials and tribulations of daily living, in the throes of larger events that shaped the world around them, and in the fortunes and misfortunes of the grand game of life.

This web of people stretches in time through many periods as well as across many places, and each person has some sense of what it means to be Peranakan in the world, each person carries a part of the Peranakan present, past and future, upon their shoulders.

Peranakan

As a social phenomenon, Peranakan society stretches across many boundaries and zones, social and ecological, and includes many different habitats and niches. Its centers can be found in different cityscapes, and its tendrils can be found stretching out into the remotest of countryside. Peranakan society may be a finite phenomenon, but its finiteness is too vast to calculate, too confusingly complex to neatly separate.

If we take as our prototypical representative of Peranakan Society, the wealthy, spoiled, elderly Nonya who has an incurable passion for gambling, chewing sireh, and hen-pecking her son-in-law, then we are leaving out too much of other Peranakan social realities—too much of its range of human variation and historical possibility. The Babas of the Seventeenth Century were clearly not the same as those of the Nineteenth Century, and these were not the same as those who claim to be so descended today.

And the urban elite of the Baba pyramid was only the somewhat ostentatious pinnacle of a larger social base—what of its more anonymous base? No History is purely a Great Man narrative—of Towkays, Kapitans, Bankers and Prime Ministers—but social history is also told of the many whose names are now forgotten, seldom remembered, but without whose combined efforts history would not have been made at all, Great or small—not even Chinese history.

Before we seek to explain Peranakan society in jargonist terms like "political economy," "social structure," "ethnicity," "pluralism," "acculturation," "assimilation," it is important to highlight several dimensions of their world that seem problematic and interesting from the standpoint of social science.

First is the apparently amazing capacity for the Peranakan to adapt to their local environment, and to take full advantage of the opportunities within this setting.

Secondly, there is the Chinese standpoint, the somewhat exceptional openness and syncretic orientation of the Peranakan culture that made of itself a curious amalgamation of different, and often contradictory, cultural models.

Finally, related to the first two points, is the somewhat ambiguous and indeterminate status of Peranakan society within a larger pluralistic world.

Peranakan society, fit within a larger framework, must be seen as both a "transitional culture" in a larger stream of cultural assimilation, and a "culture of transition" that emerged as a self-sustaining social pattern in the interstitial regions between different cultural orientations.

Peranakan culture and character emerged as a distinctive configuration wherever and whenever the processes of assimilation that were occurring in the passing of Chinese into Malay or Indonesian society were systematically arrested—incorporation into the larger, predominant host society remained incomplete and partial and was, for the most part, a relatively gradual process.

It is likely that this happened more than once, in more than one place, and that therefore the reasons for its happening were not a matter of historical happenstance, but were more structurally basic and therefore stable, such that when circumstances were ripe, the emergence of a Peranakan orientation was a little more than likely.

With its repeated occurrence, it was more than likely that these people would form distinctive communities with their own separate orientation, and that these separate communities would eventually become interlinked and interrelated to form a larger region-wide socio-cultural phenomena.

G. William Skinner speaks of a socio-historical continuum in which different Chinese communities of Indonesia "can be ranged along a gradient according to the degree of indigenous influence in their synthesized culture." (1963:104)

Position along this continuum is held to have been a function of the length of time that elapsed between the social formation of the community and the "arrival of significant numbers of immigrant China-born women.

> "The Chinese found much that was attractive and valuable in a highly differentiated, rich, complex and literate culture such as that of the Javanese, considerably less in the simpler local culture of the *Bangka*...and still less in the relatively impoverished, non-literate cultures of the Borneo aborigines." (Skinner 1963: 105)

According to Skinner, this process began in the Sixteenth Century in Java, the culture of which was stabilized by the Eighteenth Century. In Borneo and Bangka it began later in the Eighteenth Century, and a culturally distinctive local society was formed only by the mid-1800s. In other communities, such as *Bagan Siapi-api,* the process began "as late as the last decade of the nineteenth century and cultural stability is only now being achieved." (Skinner, 1963: pg. 104)

In another study, Skinner compared the differential rates of assimilation between the Chinese of Thailand and Java, who have been in both countries for similar lengths of time and who came from similar regions in China—in Thailand the rate of assimilation was three times more rapid than in Java, and

Chinese in Thailand were incorporated fully into the Thai social world by the second or third generation, and it is uncommon to find a Chinese who can trace their lineage for more than four generations, while it was not uncommon in Java to find Chinese going back twelve generations.

Skinner (G. William Skinner, 1963: pg.104-5) isolated six factors contributing to such a differential in rates of assimilation:

1. Cultural vigor, in which the unconquered Thai did not share the same "cultural inferiority," complex as did the Javanese.
2. The Thai defined themselves by culture, whereas the Javanese defined themselves by race and descent.
3. The Thai elite was indigenous and local, the elite of Java were outsiders and the Javanese upper class was deprived of any real power.
4. There was much less ethnic stratification in Thailand than in Java, in which Dutch policies ethnically stereotyped occupational categories that put the Chinese above the Javanese in socio-economic status.
5. In Thailand the Chinese were relatively unrestricted in their activities, while in Java the Dutch put restrictions on their residence and mobility.
6. Finally, in Thailand there was a recognized mechanism available to Chinese for passing from Chinese to Thai identities, in which a person, coming of age, would declare himself either under Chinese or Thai administrative control—no such mechanism for passing was available to the Chinese in Java.

According to D. E. Brown, (1976) differential rates of Chinese assimilation varied directly with rates of upward social mobility—such vertical mobility was relatively open and available to the Chinese in Thailand, making the incentive to assimilate into Thai society much greater, while in Java the ethnic hierarchy was relatively closed and fixed. Brown combines this with the promotion of "false ethnic origin stories" that perpetuate ethnic pluralism and difference, to create a general proposition that: "Ethnic diversity varies with the hereditary closure of ranking systems."

More generally, in the structural processes of Southeast Asian civilization the formation of ethnic diversity and the establishment of a fixed hierarchy were complementary and dialectical processes—"If enhancing ethnic differences promotes the stability of the radically plural society, why couldn't Southeast Asia's indigenous radically plural societies have been created by fabricating "ethnic" differentiation to complement a hierarchy which was established among essentially homogenous peoples?" (D. E. Brown, 1976:94)

Another study by Juliet Edmunds of the relationship between Islam, intermarriage and rates of assimilation between the Chinese and the Malays, notes that though Islam has been widely regarded as a significant barrier to the assimilation of the Chinese, as compared, say to Theravada Buddhism in Thailand, conversion to Islam was a process which varied historically and socially "according to the state of relations between the two groups concerned as to any theological dictates, as well as to the degree to which such conversion imposed other conditions of assimilation upon the convert." (Juliet Edmunds, 1968: pg. 57)

Intermarriage is the key element of the process of assimilation. "The effects of intermarriage on the relationships between the communities depend not only on how frequently it occurs, but also on the type of relationship and how the children of the unions are defined." (Edmunds, 1968: page 58)

Formal marriage institutionalizes the "movement of individuals from one group to another. Alternatively, they can result in the growth of some intermediate category of persons. In general it must be the host society which imposes the rules on this as well as other spheres of social life, though this does not mean that the minority, in this case the Chinese, have been entirely without a say in the process." (Edmunds: 1968: pg. 58)

In sociological jargon, intermarriage is known as the process of "amalgamation," a part of the more general processes of acculturation and social/structural assimilation. From this standpoint, Peranakan society, constituting both a transitional category in the assimilation process as well as a pariah culture of transition, may be fittingly referred to as a "culture of amalgamation."

Historically, intermarriage between Buddhist Chinese and Muslim Malays has always been infrequent, though the demographic pattern of such intermarriage has been difficult to reconstruct for a number of reasons.

Somewhat paradoxically, Peranakan society, as a culture of amalgamation, has been centrally defined by such intermarriage—

"In every case, the formative period for the locally rooted society began when immigrants settled on the land, formed alliances with indigenous women—Chinese women almost never immigrated over-seas prior to this century—and reared children who were taught to identify themselves as Chinese…Marriage among these mixed-blood descendants of immigrants led eventually to the development of a fairly stable society…" (G. William Skinner, 1963:pg. 104)

Edmunds noted that with the coming of European colonial administration, and especially with the rise of new ethnic nationalisms, the Islamic proscriptions became enforced in counter-reference to the predominantly Christian conquerors, and, combined with the emergence of strongly Nanyang immigrant Chinese communities, as well as policies promoted by both British and Dutch administrators, the barrier to intermarriage and thus assimilation of the two communities became more rigid—thus a new pariah "Peranakan" identity became established that was less 'transitional' in status.

Not every scholar unanimously supports this thesis of intermarriage as being the principle basis in the formation of Peranakan society and social identity in the Straits. John Clammer notes that lack of evidence for such intermarriage in the small pre-colonial Chinese community such as Malacca, which were internally self-sufficient and intra-communally balanced in terms of its sex ratios.

> "In fact, there is no evidence at all that Peranakan culture emerged from a process of biological syncretism; rather, it is the result of cultural assimilation and adaptation to the host country, a process which did not begin in a systematic way until the nineteenth century..."(John Clammer, 1980:46)

Clammer cites the near absolute negativity of the Islamic religion that presented a strong barrier to such intermarriage, as well as the shallowness of Peranakan lineages that do not extend back before the Nineteenth Century. He claims that Peranakan culture did not become a cohesive, internally coherent phenomenon until this time, and attributes the principal basis for its emergence as being the British colonial system that promoted their marginal pariah status.

The actual historical patterning and importance of such intermarriage has remained unresolved. There is a romantic facticity about the Peranakan origin myth of low-status Malay women marrying higher status Chinese merchants and traders and becoming the famous Nonyas who minded the store in their husbands' absence, cultivated strong domestic values and skills, nursed these values in their daughters, as well as lovingly cared for and commanded their Baba and Nonya babies, and chewed sireh and gambled among themselves in their spare time, all the while unknowing that they were sowing the seeds for what would later develop into a full blown cultural configuration.

Clammer refers to this argument, and to the Malay/Minangkabau origin of Matrilocality, as "folk arguments" that lack historical or social evidence. But this dilemma does point up the inherent ambiguity of identity of the Peranakan, of their in-betweenness, and of the possibilities, and impossibilities, of becoming either Chinese or Malay.

What remains rather certain is that at some point such intermarriage ceased fairly early, and from the standpoint of its Nonya orientation, the Peranakan society became a closed one. Chinese men and women, as well as some Malays or others, were later incorporated into its ethos, through capitalizing on the marriage market in the Straits, but the society remained otherwise separate and distinct.

———————————

Another social historical dimension of Peranakan society that may help to resolve this ambiguity of Peranakan identity is consideration of its regional/local variations and, especially, have a kind of rural-urban continuum.

In the same work, John Clammer notes the hypothesis that the "frontier conditions" of Straits society inhibited the formation of deep lineages by requiring extensive cooperation between unrelated lineage fragments. Only where such frontier conditions do not exist does patrilineal ideology and lineage become predominant. Such lineages in the South of China are also correlated with wet-rice agriculture.

According to Clammer, the urban orientation of the Peranakan as merchantmen, and the frontier conditions of Peranakan society, discouraged the development of patrilineal/patrifocal identity, and encouraged the development of the distinctive matrilocal patterns that "bias was free to flourish." (1980: pg. 39).

A number of studies have been done of rural based Peranakan communities in both Indonesia and Malaysia, and these frontier-oriented societies must be taken into account in consideration of the origin and development of Peranakan social identity.

Central in such pioneering development of the hinterland regions was the Kong Si system within which the urban based Chinese settlements financed and provided the organization and labor reserve, as well as the middle-men function and markets for the interior pioneering communities that depended upon a "slash and burn" method of shifting cultivation, nearby tropical forest exploitation, and that produced an expanding agricultural frontier.

"There is little doubt that the labourers, towkays, and financiers of individual plantations or mines had the close connexions implied in the kongsi system or that usually they were, willy-nilly, members of the same secret society. The pioneer Chinese settlements in the interior were, therefore, the frontier outposts of a closely-knit organization controlled from the Straits Settlements." (James Jackson, "Planters and Speculators: Chinese and European Agricultural Enterprise in Malaya," 1786-1921: pg. 4)

Such a system depended upon establishing trade and exchange relations and partnership based upon an ethnic Chinese ethos of reciprocal trust and the notion of dependability.

Crosscutting ties of dialect, lineage, village association, tended to reinforce these bonds, but even more importantly, kinship ties were the best available means of cementing a dependable network.

"One of the main contentions of this paper is that the Chinese were able to succeed in Vietnam because they developed mechanisms for generating interpersonal trust and regulating business behavior in the absence of a well-functioning formal legal system..." (Clifton Barton, 1983:pg. 53)

> "The Chinese approach to business was based upon personal relationships and word-of-mouth agreements. And these verbal agreements relied solely on mutual trust—*sun yung*—backed by informal group sanctions. Under these rules, if a merchant was not trustworthy and reliable, that is, if he lacked *sun yung*, it would be impossible for him to do business. Once the fact that a merchant had failed to honour his word became known, other merchants would simply refuse to do business with him." (Clifton Barton, 1983:pg. 53)

Networking is one of the most important aspects of seeing how history and culture painted with a large brush articulates with, and is moved by, the day to day interactions of individuals along their many 'pathways of practice.'

We can see Straits societies, as the pioneering forerunners of the later conglomerate Nanyang society, playing a pivotal role in the development of the Nanyang civilization in Southeast Asia. A Russian study by Simoniya of Nanyang social structure reveals a vast financial-credit-market system that extends throughout Southeast Asia, with Chinese merchant-middlemen, within a colonial and neo-colonial framework, serving as the key articulators of the entire regional political economy.

Within this system there emerges a resolute class structure in which plantation laborers and coolies are at the bottom, small petty merchants and planters range somewhere in the middle, and urban-based professionals and financiers are at the apex.

The economic stratification of Sarawak's Chinese society—or alternatively the interrelationship between rural and urban economy—is arranged like a pyramid, with a broad base of laborers and agriculturalists in rural areas: a class of rural bazaar shopkeepers in the middle, and at the apex "a small number of big businessmen and industrialists who actually control the economy... and who usually become the recognized leaders of the community." (Simoniya, 1961)

Whether in the pre-war or post-war period the economic strata in the Chinese community have stayed substantially unaltered. It is through this economic stratification that social power is channeled and leadership structure traditionally developed.

"...Because of interrelationship between rural bazaar shopkeepers and urban businessmen as between the latter and the top merchants, it can be seen that social power was channeled through the rural shopkeepers (who derived it from the grassroots agriculturalists by the granting of credits) to the urban businessmen, and again through the latter to the top merchants..."(John Chin, 1981:pg. 76-7)

As established culture brokers and as the first Chinese to settle in the Straits, the Babas emerged on top of this developing Nanyang social structure during the colonial era, and helped provide the impetus and direction for its further development. They provided the leadership and local models of adjustment and accommodation that allowed the system to work as effectively as it had.

Winzeler (1983) notes a distinction in the Kelantan region between Peranakan "village Chinese" and "town Chinese" "who perceive themselves as possessing a 'purer' model of Chinese culture. The so-called villages Chinese in general show more Malay and Thai influences in their Chinese culture. The womenfolk, for example, wear sarong although girls do wear all kinds of modern dress especially when they go to town. Like the Baba, the women also wear the Malay-style blouse called kerbaya." (Robert Winzeler, "The Ethnic Status of the Rural Chinese of the Kelantan" in The Chinese in Southeast Asia, Culture and Politics, Vol. 2,edited by L.A. Peter Gosling & Linda Y. C. Lim, Singapore: Maruzen Asia, Pte. Ltd., 1983)

> "The men folk wear sarong most of the time and in the village they usually do not wear any shirt. When they go to town they put on shirt and trousers. It is common for both men and women to carry kain batik lepas.... a long piece of cloth which women use as head scarf while men tie it around their waist or use it as head-cloth (semutar).
>
> As for food, the village Chinese eat both Malay and Thai food as well as food prepared in Chinese style. Eating with fingers is common among these Chinese." (Tan Chee Beng, "Peranakan Chinese in Northeast Kelantan" in Journal of the Malayan Branch of the Royal Asiatic Society, Vol. 55, 1982: pg. 28)

These "village Chinese" do not identify themselves as such, and, while mostly rural, have spread into the local townships and, while retaining many Malay traits, have become more urban in orientation.

Peranakan

Tan notes at some length the difficulty in finding a suitable label for these "village Chinese" whose patterns of acculturation are not quite the same as for the "Babas" of Malacca. Finally, he opts for the term "PeranakE"....

Robert Winzeler (1983) emphasizes the difference between the "rural Chinese" of Kelantan, whom he refers to as Peranakan on the basis of acculturation, and the Babas of the Straights and the Peranakan of Java. One important difference is the influence of Thai, and the intermarriage between Chinese men and Thai women.

According to Tan, early Chinese accounts of the settlements in Kelantan mention that Chinese were not permitted to marry the locals, but when they did marry, took Siamese wives. "The descendants of those early Chinese settlers who married local women had close contact with Siamese and Malays who were the majority people. This eventually led to the acculturation of the Chinese and gave rise to the formation of Peranakan Chinese society. The Peranakan Chinese culture once formed perpetuated itself until today." (Tan Chee-Beng 1981: pg. 32-3)

Another difference is linguistic—they did not speak the Baba-Malay of the Straits, but are basically bi-lingual or tri-lingual. Finally, in terms of kinship organization he notes that these communities tend to adhere toward a partilineal/patrilocal system, observing principals of adherence to surnames and surname exogamy—or 'avoidance of common surname marriage.'

Otherwise, there is little evidence to suggest "extra-familial patrilineal descent groups of a social, economic or even ritual nature." (Tan, 1981: pg. 19) He notices that kin-groups establish themselves in proximity to one another, but do not form corporate, patrilineal organizations. There is a bias towards a more bilateral pattern.

Tan's conclusions are that "close interethnic interaction in northeast Kelantan is the main factor for good interethnic relationship and the acculturation of the Chinese. Interethnic socialization from childhood to adulthood has fostered a greater interethnic understanding and respect. As a result of such socialization, members of different ethnic groups have developed certain common values and "cultural taste."

At the group level, he notes the persistence of "'structural" contradictions that tended to maintain group boundaries between the rural Chinese and the Malays. Overtly, the Peranakan Chinese appear more Malay than Chinese because of their dress and language, "which are exhibited everyday, are very much acculturated" (Tan, 1981: pg. 48), "but on close scrutiny, they remain basically Chinese in orientation. "Interestingly, it is in the area of religious differences, and syncretism, that the strongest basis for difference and identity are to be found."

L. A. P. Gosling's study on the rural Chinese of Terengganu (1964) whom he calls "Baba Chinese" focuses upon the pattern of pioneering settlement in the region by rural Chinese. Those Chinese who remained behind in settlements and did not move on to greener pastures, or those settlements that proved unsuccessful, were fully incorporated by the Malays.

According to Gosling, "Baba Chinese was "used in recognition of the popular usage of the term to apply to all Chinese in Malaya displaying a significant level of cultural and biological assimilation" (Gosling, 1964: pg. 203)

Gosling cites that among the rural Malays, there were few if any significant barriers of Islam to intermarriage. "Malay marriage partners were not difficult to obtain. The details of Islamic law were not well known to the rural Malays, and prohibition on marriage between Muslim Malay women and pagan Baba Chinese males does not seem to have been strictly applied." (Ibid, 1983: pg. 215)

While most such intermarriage involved the incorporation of females into the Baba community, there was also a lesser reverse flow of Chinese into the Malay community, as households remained behind in the advance of the Chinese settlements, and became incorporated by the local Malays who were more sedentary in orientation. Babas could easily assimilate into the Malay communities because they were already partly acculturated "in physical appearance, language, costume, and behaviour." (Ibid. 1983: pg. 217)

Furthermore, a premium may have been placed upon lighter complexioned Chinese Babas. In terms of physical appearance, which Gosling takes as primary evidence for such biological assimilation, the Baba Chinese varied over a wide range between Malay and Chinese. Older generation individuals looked more Malay in appearance. He advanced the hypothesis that areas most visible to external contact are the most acculturated, while the least visible areas showed least evidence of acculturation.

Acculturation seems also to have been a function of the relative isolation of the Chinese communities and members from other Chinese—attenuated contacts in rural areas, promoted more contact with the local, host society. On the other, the onward resettlement of some Chinese tended to isolate these communities from contact with the Malays, thus reducing the amount of assimilation. Gosling divides the history of these settlements into three periods.

The first, from 1820 until 1890, was a period of growth, "and the process of acculturation and biological assimilation proceeded rapidly" (1964: pg. 215). The second period, between 1890 and 1920, is one marked by declining population, during which Babas were increasingly assimilated into surrounding Malay communities.

From 1920 until the present, assimilation into the Malay communities has been all but completely arrested, and the size of the Baba community, identified as distinctly Peranakan, has stabilized. There is recent evidence to suggest a more recent trend of resinification by a larger Chinese community.

Social stratification exists within, defines, and is defined by, a continuum of social interaction, enduring relations and interpersonal experience that exist throughout time and across space. Social stratification is transmitted through the generations and between different groupings and sub-groupings. It delimits group boundaries and asymmetries of power, and, in the sense of transcending the lived experience of any single individual, must be considered to be "corporate" in structure.

Social stratification can be seen to underlie ethnic stratification, boundaries, groups and identities. Just as social stratification varies through time and across space, so too does ethnic differences vary continuously in a corresponding way. Such continuous variation is the basis for speaking of an ethno-cultural continuum of human experience.

It sometimes happens, as in the cases of radically plural societies, that ethnic stratification becomes the defining principle of social stratification, with the resulting "ethos of ethnos." In such cases, ethnic differences and ethnic identities come to take on a social significance, and a real potency, which they might not otherwise have had. Also, defining social ethos in primarily in terms of "ethnos" tends to constrain and shape its patterning in ways which it might not have otherwise been shaped.

Peranakan

Though perhaps inextricably interrelated, the two kinds of phenomena—social stratification and ethnic stratification—are yet separable and potentially independent processes. Socio-cultural homogeneity within a society may preclude some of the organizational problems that ethnic heterogeneity causes, and ethno-cultural differences also entail its own kinds of dilemmas. Yet stratification occurs in either case, and in neither case does such homogeneity or heterogeneity preclude the potential for competition and conflict on the one hand, or cooperation and social integration on the other.

Within the colonial framework of a plural society, immigrant Chinese communities were divided along sub-ethnic lines in both cooperation and competition—sub-ethnic identity delimited the field of opportunities and actions open to the immigrant. Although internal class distinctions existed, these were of far less significance in daily life than ethnic solidarity. "In sum, cleavages and alliances within Chinese immigrant society were both complex and of daily significance, whereas for all but the elite, contacts between Malays and with Europeans were few and relatively unimportant." (Gosling, 1983: pg. 242)

In a landmark study in reference group theory, Alvin Rabushka's work Race and Politics in Urban Malaya (1973) reveals some of the fundamental differences between Chinese and Malay. Chinese tend to be more culturally ethnocentric than the Malay.

More cosmopolitan contexts, inducing social extroversion, hence greater interracial social interaction, reduces such ethnocentrism, while social introverts tend to be much more ethnocentric in orientation.

In terms of relative social distance, and the degree of tolerance between these groups, "Penang Malays are more tolerant of the Chinese than their Kuala Lumpur counterparts, but they are less tolerant on the question of interracial marriage. But omitting eating and marriage, the two associations affected by religion, we find (with one exception) that two-thirds of all Malay respondents are not opposed to crossing racial boundaries in employment, social activity or neighborhood of residence." (Rabushka, 1973: pg. 62)

In regard to Chinese attitudes, no religious obstacles interfere with Chinese eating with Malays in the same eating-houses. "Chinese in both Kuala Lumpur and Penang are more tolerant of Malays than Malays are tolerant of them. In greater degree, they are willing to eat, work, joining and live with members of the Malay race." (Ibid, 1973: 62) The study holds that racial stereotypes have little or no role in promoting social or political harmony, and that positive or negative attitudes were relatively independent of such stereotypes.

Malay stereotypes of the Chinese are that they are intelligent, ambitious, active, honest, thrifty, industrious, and hardworking, yet ritually unclean and impure. The Chinese tend to see the Malays as clean, and yet lacking ambition, while "Intelligence, thrift, activity, and honesty are given approximately equal point values... and fall significantly below the scores registered for cleanliness and (lack of) ambition." (Alvin Rabushka, 1973: 67)

Rabushka considers such stereotypes as economical means for storing large amounts of information, which might otherwise be costly. Stereotypes do not vary in relation with social introversion/extroversion and are not correlated with expressed attitudes of willingness to interact. "...The holding of narrow stereotyped views in Malaya has no visible impact on either social interchange or political unity." (Ibid, pg. 67)

From these findings, a conclusion is drawn, among others, that "multi-racial living experiences do not necessarily promote racial tolerance or political unity" (Ibid, pg. 101) The data tended to support a "transaction hypothesis" that higher levels of daily social interaction tended to promote higher levels of positive effect.

On the other hand, evidence points out that social integration does not necessarily correlate with "democratic political stability"—"the transaction model does not clearly distinguish the political and nonpolitical aspects of "integration." Living in multiracial neighborhoods increases affect, whereas ethnic enclaves reduce it. Education enhances interethnic interaction, while age, religious and sexual differences have little impact "on the extent of racial integration." (Ibid, pg. 124-5)

Non-Baba Chinese look down upon Babas because they do not speak well the Chinese language—they are perceived "as not quite Chinese," and as "like Malay," which for the Non-Baba Chinese is a counter-reference group. Those who speak English, the language of an ascendant reference group, are more acceptable—this category crosscut the Baba-Non-Baba distinction. Outside of the Baba areas, there is not a great deal of understanding of their ethnic culture— when seen buying pork in the market, they are frequently mistaken for being Malay. (Tan Chee-Beng, 1979: pg. 21) Non-Baba Chinese may call them "*Baba siau*"—a derogatory name meaning "Baba semen"—and "*Baba kia*" meaning "Baba kids." Babas often experience direct insults by Non-Babas in many social contexts. Babas complain that they are looked down upon by the Non-Babas.

Baba Chinese, on the other hand, have traditionally looked down upon the *Singkehs*, or newcomers, who in an earlier period were generally poor coolie laborers. "*Cinageh*" is heard among Babas when they talk unfavorably of non-Baba Chinese.

Nevertheless, in reference to a host Malay community, both Babas and non-Baba's share a common sense of Chineseness, a common Chinese cultural core, a common religious orientation, and a common ethnic and existential context of structural and social discrimination. "Now the common perception of discrimination unites the Babas and the non-Baba Chinese in a common political sentiment." (Tan Chee Beng, 1979:22)

They also share as certain degree of social relatedness—marriage across these sub-ethnic boundaries is quite common and normally unconstrained, in which extended kinship alliances can be cultivated. Such kinship linkages extend to "ritual kinship"—adoption of a child by a Godmother or Godfather.

My wife took me to see her God-mum, whom she called "Lau Mak" which means "old Mom", an old Cantonese woman who was her amah as a child—she was the only person who gave us <u>ang-pao</u> (red envelopes with money) and ritual offerings for our wedding. Religious ceremonies and rituals are an important means and locus of such sub-ethnic interaction that helps to define and reinforce a common "Chinese" identity.

Non-Baba Chinese frequently disdain Malays, and completely avoid them. They are seen as untrustworthy and are not extended credit. They feel Malays "are decidedly different from themselves in ways of thinking and feeling—*xinli butong*—and the assumption seems to be that the differences are irreconcilable." (Judith Strauch, 1981: 254)

Chinese tend to see Malay behavior in the local context as childlike, with a lack of ambition—"traits that can be smiled on with some condescension" (Ibid. pg. 254) These attitudes are somewhat separate from feelings of structural discrimination as "second class citizens". "Government officials, by contrast, may be viewed as heavy-handed tyrants spoon-feeding the Malay peasant on the one hand and constricting natural Chinese rights on the other." (Ibid, pg. 254)

According to Judith Nagata, though there is a great deal of irregular subethnic diversity, the most salient element of Malay ethnic identity is cultural—"a Malay is a Muslim, habitually speaks the Malay language, and follows Malay adat, or customary law." (Nagata, 1974:335)

Malay Muslims, whether Malay, Arabic or Indian, situationally defines themselves according to different reference groups varying along three dimensions: simple comparison of social distance and solidarity; immediate expediency; and normative statements regarding comparative values of social status. (Nagata, 1974: 340; In Judith Strauch, 1979:256)

Individuals may oscillate flexibly between identities without negative psychological or social consequences—such oscillation may be both personally and socially adaptive.

In terms of interaction between Babas and Malays, the same perceptual categories of inferiority do not hold—rather stereotypes are common that contain negative and positive attributes.

From the standpoint of Non-Baba Chinese, both Babas who are "like Malays" and Malays, are often seen as less hard working or industrious that the Chinese—a core value of Chinese-ness.

"Neither are Malays seen as trustworthy—such trust in business interaction being another central tenet in the economic underpinnings of ethnic Chinese identity. For the Baba community, if they identify more strongly with the Chinese, then they are apt to view the Malay in similar terms — if they identify more with a separate Baba identity, they are apt to distinguish themselves from the Chinese and identify more strongly with the Malays." (Tan Chee-Beng, 1979: pg. 25)

"Malays, when questioned about their perception of the identity of the Babas, will often reply that: 'They are just like us.'" (John Clammer, 1980: pg. 133)

Babas interact more closely and frequently with Malays, than do other Chinese, and yet they are separate in the spheres of kinship and religion from the Malay — spheres which they share with other Chinese. Malays perceive the Babas as easier to interact with than the Non-Baba Chinese.

On the other hand, many Peranakan have picked up many values and views which can be considered traditionally Malay, such as the distinction between refined, "*alus*" or "*halus*" and rough or crude, or "*kasar*" — a distinction that is brought out in the way that a Peranakan may speak to another depending upon the social category that the Peranakan identifies the person with. Also, Nonyas have picked up many of the superstitions that were Malay — I have frequently heard my wife say under her breath "I *'pantang'* that" only to learn later that it meant a strong "dislike," and specifically, an omen of ill-fortune.

In spite of the structural differences between the two communities, there still exist many interethnic social ties between them — people are customarily invited to and attend friends weddings, parties, and ceremonies as a token of interethnic solidarity. In such situations, discussion of issues of structural discrimination or difference may be avoided or else joked about.

"This points to the fact that where there is structural
conflict between two ethnic groups in a multi-ethnic
country, the interaction between individuals of the two
ethnic groups need not necessarily manifest conflict."
(Tan Chee-Beng, 1979: pg. 27)

In such multi-ethnic conflicts, certain norms, of avoidance, of
not offering pork for instance, are mutually worked out to
smooth interpersonal social interaction in the wake of
structural difference and inequality. To some extent, personal
identity is separate and independent of ethnic-group identity.

We are left to consider "ethnos" as a function of "reference"
and as such subject to an intrinsic kind of psychological and
social relativity of our self-awareness in relation to others.
Identity is built up from enduring social interrelation and
frequent social interaction.

In this sense, the psychological awareness of the self and
the social perception of others are inextricably entangled,
and overlap in an intermediate region that is not quite internal
and not completely external.

In this sense, relative deprivation, cognitive dissonance, and
perceived social difference and distance, are all phenomena
that have both psychological and sociological facets in
experience. In this regard, status-role ascription,
identification, projection of "collective representations"—all
symbolic processes—and labeling, serve to reinforce and
articulate this region of inter-ethnic, psycho-social
consciousness, resorting to stereotyped ethnic descriptions
and epithets.

V: The Social World of the Straits Chinese

"All societies are, in a radical sense, plural societies."
(A.F.C. Wallace, <u>Culture and Personality</u> 1970:109-110)

I have in my research on the Peranakan found very little directly and explicitly describing the social structure and organizational patterns of Straits Chinese society. Perhaps the most descriptive account was an interesting study of the late 19th Century was that written by J. D. Vaughan (<u>The Manners and Customs of the Chinese of the Sraits Settlements</u>, 1879, reprinted 1971)

Much of the literature presumes either an endless beginning—as if the Peranakan of the original old Malacca in the 15th Century were somehow the same as those of the new Malacca of the 20th Century, even after an estimated thirty generations of descendants (less or more,) from which we could validly conclude that in a half a Millennium there issued literally thousands of Baba and Nonya descendants.

Or else we just imagine the Peranakan locked in an endless, frozen present, where all change is cyclical and generations repeat themselves fundamentally unchanged in core and spirit every twenty years or so, or at least five times per Century.

Even so, whether they were the original founders of Malacca, or those Malaccan Chinese under the Dutch and then the English, or those of the Modern era, we know nothing directly with so little first-hand evidence, in order to better understand the social conditions and historical processes that made them what they were and what they became through those five Centuries of cultural survival and change.

Presumably, what it looked like under the original Chinese sailors, officials and traders of Admiral Cheng Ho's expeditions, with Malacca becoming as a protectorate and state of Ming China, was not how Straits Chinese Society may have looked under the Portuguese during the time of the Malacca Sultanate, and their many battles and wars with neighboring sultanates.

This is the case much more under the Dutch allied with the Sultan of Johor with their emphasis upon spice and plantation trade, or then under the British, or even the late-arriving military and administrative, and mostly racist, representatives of Japanese Empire. We have the following estimates of generations of Baba and Nonya descendants:

1. Pre-Chinese Sultanate of Malacca—Baseline.
2. Ming Chinese Traders and Settlers. (1405-1511, 106 years, approximately 5 generations.)
3. Portuguese (1511-1641, 130 years, or about six generations.) This era was marked by chronic warfare with the Sultanates by the Portuguese defenders and Portuguese interests in the exotic spice trade.
4. The Dutch in Malacca during the second half of the 17th Century and most of 18th Centuries (1641-1824), before ceding the city to the British as a result of the almost 183 years (approximately 8-9 generations) of intermittent Dutch occupation. Growth of cash crop plantations.
5. The British administration of Malacca, by the beginning of the 19th Century until independence (British ruled Malacca during the Napoleonic era between 1795 and 1818, or about one generation)
6. The Dutch resumed control of Malacca in 1818 until the Anglo-Dutch treaty gave control of Malacca back to the British in 1825. (.33 generation of Dutch Administration.

British empowered the Chinese and fought the Chinese secret societies.

7. British control resumed after Anglo-Dutch Treaty of 1825, lasting until Japanese period of occupation (120 years; about 5 generations) that was marked by massive importation of Chinese coolie labor.
8. Japanese control: 4 years, or .25 generation)
9. Resumption of British control over Malayan Peninsula between 1945 and 1957. (.5 generation)
10. Modern National Era: 1957 to Present (66 years, about 3 generations.)

It is evident that the Straits Chinese Society grew substantially under both the Dutch and the British, and from commencement of Japanese administrative occupation marked the zenith and subsequent eclipse of Peranakan cultural development in increasing competition with other ethno-cultural and ethno-national identities.

It seems likely to have been the case that the rapid generational growth of Malayan Chinese populations was a consequence overall of high birth rates as well as high infant mortality rates, with probably marriage of young Nonya's by their 18th Birthday.

If this were the case, the fuel for expansion of these communities would have been the importation of Chinese labor (predominantly male) from the Mainland or other communities throughout the Nanyang economic empire, and an emphasis upon retention of women and upon their domestic and reproductive functions in the household.

Few Muslim Malay women would have crossed that ethnocultural and ethno-religious boundary within tradition bound and highly conservative societies. While Chinese men may have crossed the boundary into Malayan Muslim society, probably few Malay men crossed into the Straits

Chinese world through marriage. Peranakan Chinese females would have ended up marrying within and often downwardly of the diaspora Chinese community of excess young males. But these young males would be brought into the wife's lineage if they demonstrated desirable of hard work, constancy and filial piety.

In essence, each of these periods of time, from the original Chinese founders, through the Portuguese, Dutch, British and Modern Era constitutes five or six distinct periods of Peranakan history.

Counting three generations of the modern era, an approximate total of about 28-30 (twenty year) generations of Chinese Peranakan were born within or probably associated with Malacca and the emerging Straits Settlements since the baseline of its formal founding—and probably much deeper and longer if we go back to the earlier Sultanate of Malacca Era.

The Portuguese compounded themselves into the fort they had built at Malacca, and, having antagonized the Malay Sultans, were repeatedly attacked by coalition forces, even the Chinese from China, for which Malacca under the Sultanate and Chinese had been a tributary trade state and protectorate of the Ch'ing Chinese Empire.

Chinese traders came to boycott Malacca, and Portuguese habits and practices in slaving, quest for transportable wealth (gold, silver, exotic tropical products) and militant coercion tended to channel trade to other ports and quays, resulting in the development of extensive trade networks not including Malacca.

The Dutch conquest of Malacca resulted in the withdrawal of the Portuguese, and the rise to power of the Sultanate of Johor. The Dutch had next to little interest in territorial dominion, but rather control of coastal nexus points for the promotion of trade, and held greater, more valuable trading interests in other areas of the larger Nusantera.

The Dutch were known, as elsewhere like Ceylon, to wage war systematically not only against their European competitors like the less organized Portuguese, the French and the British, but also to systematically fight hostile indigenous tribes in alliance with indigenous people who supported and traded with the Dutch. Nor were the Dutch completely immune to miscegenation and the siring of respectable "*Kristang*" half-breed families.

Chinese interests had been during this 18th Century Era in mining along the coasts of Sarawak (gold and bauxite) and plantations in the coastal areas of Johor, including Gambier, black pepper, often traded to China, betel nut, and clove, as well as the mining of tin upon the Peninsula. This interest led Chinese to establish plantations in black pepper and Gambier in Johor under the Kangcha cash-crop system.

This cash-crop plantation system developed along the rivers in Johor under the Dutch presumably during the late 17th and 18th Centuries, and soon became associated with development of clan associations, "Kong si's" or "Grandfather or Lineage Organizations" as well as the affiliated secret society networks that protected and promoted different and competing clan or dialect or ethnocultural networks.

These diagonalized organizations provided a source of cheap and cooperative labor, often indentured by irrecoverable debts, as well as coercive authority and potential depredation and conflict between these horizontally-diagonally stratified organizations of the radically plural, diaspora societies within a dominant host state or provincial system

Peranakan

The Kangcha system and its description in association with organization of Chinese labor, trade systems, consociation with Malay Sultans, and emergence of benevolent and secret societies, largely associated with the Straits Settlements, marks the first known records of distinct Straits Chinese Society that probably had its original birth and developmental origin before the arrival of the Chinese under Admiral Cheng Ho.

Patterns consistent to this Overseas Chinese Society would probably have been something like the following:

1. Attempts to create an alternative Chinese-style sense of civilization within patrilineal system as the "dominant or preferred" modality of the Nanyang Chinese, resulting in clan-based social organization.
2. The numbers of Chinese and lack of land holding within the semi-confederated Malay states would have never been sufficient for achieving political dominance except in very local contexts, rendering the Chinese modality subordinate to the Malay (and then subsequent European) modalities, with the rise of alternative sub-modalities and proliferation of para-potent Chinese secret society and clan organizations across these multiple ethnocultural sub-modalities.
3. Within such a system, highly adaptive to shifting political circumstances, and developmentally evolving with each new set of acculturative and amalgamative pressures and influences, a predominant socio-political system based upon cooperative-competitive and complementative relations would develop in which balance of power was achieved through alliance and coalition and tethered together through socio-economic trade networks of which the Overseas Chinese mediated, monopolized and exploited to their own economic and social success in status mobility.

4. This may have lead to the following marriage patterns determining presence or prevalence of matrilocal residence.
   a. Chinese men taking Chinese Peranakan wives and retaining Chinese religion.
   b. Non-Chinese wives of Chinese men would set up domestic arrangements devoted to the up bringing of "half caste" children.
   c. Chinese husbands of Malay Muslim wives would convert to Islam, at least nominally, and move to the margins of Straits Chinese ethnoculture (part of a larger Me'tis Chinese Peranakan ethnoculture.)
5. The resulting cultural amalgamation would result in further proliferation of alternative ethnocultural "sub-modalities" that were probably quite flexible into fitting within and adapting to local and regional socio-structural systems.
6. The center of these communities was local, and they networked with other similar communities at increasing distance within the Nanyang trade empire.
7. These adaptations would focus on local exploitation, pioneering development, and trade and the handling and exchange and transfer of goods, gold and money.
8. A baseline and often underground consequence of these arrangements within colonial society would have been formation of enduring and highly dynamic network patterns involving sodalities within which external resources would be made available, including trade and work associations, benevolent societies, "grandfather organizations (Kong Si's) and secret societies and gangs formed around work, trades, and clans.

There are comparative case-models and principles of social structure to be applied, at least in part, in venturing to hypothesize what that Straits Chinese social structure may have looked like, well before the beginning of the 20th Century.

It can be presumed that the original pattern of immigration of Chinese men to Malacca, and presumably elsewhere in the region, relied for success in trade on local and long distance marriage alliances, not just with any Malay female or other woman, "prostitute or slave," but one maybe born and raised into the local leadership or even the princely "*alus*" class.

It may well be that a Chinese princess came to early Malacca with some few hundred retainers who ended up marrying local, mostly Chinese men. This event alone would in 30 generations have produced tens of thousands of contemporary Peranakan descendants, at least.

Before the arrival of the Chinese Princess, presumably the Chinese population of Malacca was primarily men, and any coolie laborers, crafts people or traders, found themselves working plantations or venturing into forests for exotic and highly prized products, establishing shop-houses where the ground floor or front-end was articulated to the outside world for business transaction, and the upper floor or backend presumably reserved for family and some nominal sense of privacy.

Many of these Chinese men would have taken wives and made large families, and many of them were probably drawn into the local social and cultural frameworks around the Kampong, the Chinese village or shop/clan district, or the mosque or temple, frequently converting to Islam as a requirement of marriage and acceptance into these communities.

I believe many of these young ladies may have been daughters of the local village *Penghulu*, or headman, or better yet, of the district or provincial *Datuk*, who would have had near absolute authority over his subjects within his small realm.

This in turn entailed that Chinese men could elevate their status and stature in the new world, and thus gained an opportunity perhaps to reinvent their identities based on local native or European standards (or both sets simultaneously).

Successful and reliable long-distance trade networks and negotiations depended upon developing ties of family and kinship into those societies that could control both regional ends of long-distance the forest-product and spice trade that was the main interest of the Dutch within the framework of the Dutch East India Company.

If a product could not be had or found locally, it may be found remotely and acquired through these long-distance networks, however many intermediate hands the product had to pass through, all at some nominal cost.

This led to the perceived and eventually received stereotype of the stingy, exploitative, non-generous, socially closed, clannish and money-faced Chinese involved and preoccupied with counting small money and some, often polytypical form of merchant business engagement.

The ethos of the Chinese was not directly the pinching of pennies or the exploitation of customers, but in general selling and moving merchandise, as cheaply or as dearly as possible, as long as the merchandise moved to the satisfaction of the customer and the rule of "absolutely no returns or refunds" was observed. In other words, "buyer beware and buy ONLY at one's own risk."

This in turn begot the stereotype of the "Cheap Chinese" counting pennies and hoarding their cash (largely true with significant exceptions of the preoccupation with gambling, risk taking investment, and ostentatious displays of fireworks and fineries and plenty of food during significant holiday or familial/community celebrations.

Business and informal money-handling practices of which Chinese gained a very early education and expertise, probably resulted in the counter-reference stereotype of "a fool and their money are soon parted," and hence fostering a social boundary of impersonalness, closure, ingenuity and greediness even before community service or support.

What we can call the dominant cultural modality of the early Nanyang Chinese Peranakan was the Chinese lineage system as a universal framework, a model, for the state.

The clan system that they would have adopted was how they constructed their world in which traditional religious authority built upon reinforcement of patrilineal structure base upon surname exogamy in closed clan (horizontally) stratified social structure, skewed diagonally through continuous and omnipresent adaptation within radically plural host societies, combined effectively with the contagious authority of a crowd organized on the basis of a hierarchy of familial classification.

The Chinese settlers brought with them their patrilineal social structure and undoubtedly created their own clan system, but they could articulate this clan structure quite flexibly within an overarching traditional system of hereditary and obligatory entitlement, to which they were foreign and peripheral guest.

It is doubted that great amounts of Chinese labor came into the Straits settlements in the earliest era, but it is also the case that the Chinese organized themselves into their own clan-based social system centered around their ethnic neighborhoods, often craft or labor specialized, and the segregation and separation of which was important to the Dutch sense of urban planning and socio-political control.

New-born children soon coming of age within a decade or two, educated in family business as well as in ethnocultural values, norms and expectations, would have been the primary source of growth of these communities, while immigrants coming from China or elsewhere would have served to fill and keep full the bottom tiers of that society.

It was precisely the flexibility of the Chinese kin-centric system of social organization, and its fundamental embedding in Chinese ethnocultural worldview, that permitted that system to function successfully under multiple overlapping and often conflicting hierarchies.

The traditional hierarchy of the aristocratic Royal Malay princes and Sultans, who would have been the primary source of the provisioning and tasking of labor in the early exotic products production and trade, and under the Dutch who provided the political and military and administrative control of the region for the sake of this trade.

In such a system, the Kin-centric nature of clan-based organization as a dominant modality with substantial variability entailed a compatibility with host lineages and family systems, and made marriage an important foundation for amalgamation, in making a living and rearing children.

Marriage to a successful Chinese brought probably some sense of special status and probably brought comparative wealth into one's family nexus. The critical difference between the two would have been the Hawaiian versus Sudanese Kinship systems, with an overlay upon the former Malay system of surname endogamy with broadened, overlapping and fewer categories of affinal and consanguineal relatives, while the latter Chinese based system would have been more open to partner exchange through clan-based surname exogamy.

Peranakan

Both systems permitted and probably promoted one way or another polygyny where and whenever multiple women would have been available, and multiple wives would have been regarded both as a source of heartache and competition, but also as a sign of social status.

In the practice of clan exogamy, sometimes becoming ethno-cultural exogamy, presumably the early Chinese kinship system was running up against the basically Hawaiian Kinship system of the Malays and other indigenous peoples to the Malaccan Straits, (possibly the *Minangkabau* for instance.)

The two systems were traditionally and religiously focused upon family construction, development and preservation in a traditional as well as practical sense, but the latter system permitted greater play of women within village and social contexts, and greater sense of shared equality, which from a Baba-Nonya point-of-view entailed a sense of relationship with one's in-laws.

The great flexibility of the Chinese clan system, in adaptation to local circumstances, provided a dominant socio-cultural modality allowing itself to subordinate itself to native dominant and European dominant modalities, and yet to function productively and profitably to the mutual benefit of others. This permitted an accommodation of traditional rules to fit local conditions, that meant among other things marriage to partners across clan and tribal boundaries.

Chinese Clan System in SEA Context

Overseas Chinese have traditionally relied upon variations of a clan-based social structure, inherited from Old China, and these were essentially replicated wherever the old-fashioned Chinese diaspora could be found with a density greater than a single Chinese family within a five-mile radius.

The isolating, componential and Sudanese "Isolating" kinship system of the Chinese, providing as discrete a category and label as the most possible to discrete intra-familial relations within three generations, as well as providing a framework for "inter-familial" relations through marriage based upon surname exogamy and bride-price, could be said to reinforce and provide a foundation for the sub-ethnic categories and criteria of reckoning between many different Chinese by degrees of affinity/proximity, fictive assigned identity, and implied trustworthiness.

This is largely a social ego function, but it also translates through the socio-centric, Sino-centric orientation of the Chinese to attitudes and bonds of solidarity, ethno-identity and sense of pride, however ethnocentric this may really be.

If the Chinese may be strongly ethnocentric in orientation (I believe them on average to be thus) they are also not particularly egocentric, quite unlike their American counterparts, and are part of a collectivist culture that devalues marked egocentrism and strong emotional expression of character.

Replacing a strongly socio-centric orientation in getting along with others especially upon a face-to-face basis, Chinese will adopt very practical attitudes and approaches to dealing with others, and not assume a moral chip on the shoulder or high-ground unlike their American counterparts, well known abroad for their cross-cultural hypocrisies.

This ancestral homeland in Old China, dialect group, lineage surname, trade-association, membership to a Chinese benevolent society, all become important criteria in the vast accounting system that has been and that had made Chinese civilization what it has been in the world—closed, clannish and mysterious from the outside looking in.

Wherever Chinese may go and be as sojourners or middlemen, there are always local people of many different persuasions whom they may or may not trust, situationally at least, but as long as there are one or more other proximate Chinese in the context, these will automatically be the ones whom to go to if there is any true support and reciprocity to be had.

From a traditional Chinese point of view this sense of long-distance trust is not only fundamental in Chinese social dynamics, but therefore relatively inviolable where violation is basically tabooed as an irreparable "loss of face" and hence a significant diminishing of one's social status identity.

This is why transactional dealings in Chinese society was often "two-faced" in the sense that what happened in public settings as a matter of ritual formalism, politeness and manners, versus what happens in the background, rendering the appearance of polite formalism and courtesy with the main function to distract and obstruct observation of what may really be going on discrepantly in the background.

Undoubtedly this entails some degree of emotional and psychosocial splitting of self-identity, in the Chinese case consumed within the social nexus as primary reference points, as well as a degree of social behavioral compartmentalization.

This structure could be modified at the ground and community level to fit various dominant socio-structural "modalities," whether Portuguese, Dutch or British colonial authorities, or else traditional local or higher level *Datuks* and *Penghulus* and their kampong villagers.

This clan-based alternate modality framework provided a highly adaptive structure that could be thus adjusted and modified broadly in the interpretation of relative statuses, roles and expectations of reciprocities.

Even more importantly, this type of social organization for which the Chinese were built by Confucius, their history and heritage, permitted the formal and legitimate cover of a public front end that served as an effective screen disguising network relations and transactions out the backend that may have been considered suspicious or nefarious, and that came to be organized on a quasi-paralegal and "criminal" perspective as Chinese gangs and secret society organization.

This pattern, of infusing diagonal and horizontal sodalities (club or gang like associations based upon shared fictive identities and traits) crisscrossed network fashion even over entire Oceans, much less over mountains or across rivers or valleys in the interior, within nested umbrella structures of relative politically dominant modalities.

These networks served to function as a normal and normally disguised social screen, acting within a single community and across similar communities, somewhat like a long soap molecule, in which one end sticks to water and the other end sticks to grease.

The end fostering a received and perceived sense of legitimacy provides not only a covering screen for pursuit of other potentially suspect interests, which are completely normalized, but more importantly also providing viable network opportunities for extending these back-end networks well up and out of the immediate, local sub-world into a larger world beyond.

Under multiple protective umbrellas, these clan-based communities and their members nested themselves up under multiple modalities or alternative socio-cultural hierarchies and their constructive symbolic behavioral cultures.

These nested modalities served as umbrellas screening external or higher formal observation of activities and conduct of business that suited Chinese interests and that fit their worldview and religion in the gambling and playing of numbers and praying on ritual daily rounds for health, wealth and good fortune.

This provided long-distance resources, opportunities, markets and leverage not only to pirates and smugglers, sailors and fishermen, but also to gangsters, secret society members, Kong-si clansmen, Association members, Chinese communist and nationalist radicals alike, as well as to normal businessmen in small localized shop-house districts who might be in need of a supplementary income at relatively long distance.

Not only did this system, flexible in its adjustments, non-ideologically aligned except through Chinese religionism, provide the necessary social "tunneling" capacity for the broad, replete and multilayered extension of informal Chinese networks, or sodalities, crosscutting the hierarchy of nested modalities governing the greater state society.

It also provided a framework for creating a system in which different modalities came to effectively compete and yet cooperate with one another without complete complementation (closed competition) occurring, stabilizing a political system otherwise inherently weak at the top.

Besides their proverbial and somewhat colloquial work ethic, that made the Chinese out to be competitive threats to almost every other ethnic group, higher-level regime authorities appreciated the Chinese for their demonstrations and measure of conventionalism, conformity and obedience.

Chinese in their clan style society were also by and large considered a productive stabilizing influence that the members provided as merchant middlemen and pariah capitalists in an otherwise shaky system of plural relationships and interactions.

Except for the depredations of their secret societies, functioning through smuggling, blackmail, extortion through coercive threats, occasional fires or murders, kidnapping, theft, trafficking in drugs, distributing opium, running prostitution, etc. They appreciated them for their magical capacity to mobilize workers or protestors or fighters or demonstrators.

Colonial authorities over states and localities such as the Straits Settlements were most likely, most of the time, de facto weak in their capacity to provide day-to-day authority and enforcement of laws and rules especially in plural and semi-rural contexts in which laws and rules were in essence configured under multiple alternative and never unchallenged mixed authorities that derived from alternative sources and fundamentally represented the friction-generating interaction of non-compatible and often contradictory systems.

A part of this was the Clan Chinese capacity to rapidly mobilize human resources at single points of place and time, drawing human power from both diagonal frameworks that included many vertical and horizontal linkages in their networking prowess.

Undoubtedly colonial authorities of whichever states came to rely upon this kind of mobilization orchestrated under the Chinese shadow for the sake of prosecuting war and managing crowds and conflict, or more commonly for the unloading of a cargo ship or the regular portage of contraband goods over a sometimes treacherous jungle trail.

In this we can see to facets of the Babas and Nonyas, and the roles of other Peranakan peoples throughout most of not all the nation-states of Southeast Asia. They early on effectively bridged the gaps between colonial and indigenous people and their alternative socio-structural and symbolic systems.

In the early stages, relative Chinese to non-Chinese population ratios were low enough, that Chinese experienced significant native assimilation, amalgamation, including inter-marriage, and accommodation.

They experienced a similar thing in the other direction of creolization and adoption of an "acro-culture" that resembled the reigning plenipotent, yet lacking clear unambiguous or total authority not articulated through pariah middle-man minority leadership, by successive foreign Colonial administrations.

Peranakan

The domestication of the Nonya female as the "keeper of the keys" to the inner sanctums of the Baba world order served the purpose of protecting the key to the Straits Chinese future, and that defined in lineage terms as the reproduction of children and the increase in ratios to a significant population size a Peranakan community.

If Chinese females in these communities were relatively scarce "commodities" up until the late 19th Century at least, with gradually rising female populations rising throughout the 19th Century under divided British and Dutch control of the Nusantera, then the reproductive function of these fully domesticated women would be protected and put at a premium, as evidenced by their displays of wealth and leisure preoccupations.

The Baba communities, once well established and fairly well rooted to the soil of their settlements in Singapore, Malacca, Georgetown and Province Wellesley, probably generated their own population growth, as did the other Overseas Chinese of the neighboring communities.

Between 1900 and 1925, Straits Chinese settlements in the Malayan Peninsula, and probably long the river deltas of the western and northern coasts of Borneo, Chinese population growth in these communities, almost completely provided through the British era "credit-ticket" system, and across Malayan territories, reached almost fifty percent of the national population in relation to the Malays and Indian resident populations.

At the same time, the number of Chinese women immigrating to these settlements as domestic labor primarily also significantly increased to become more balanced in sex-ratios.

It was likely that traditional Baba communities, built on a modified clan-based system, were as much in danger of being ethno-culturally swamped by the rapidly growing Overseas Chinese diaspora populations under the British, with their rubber, copra, tea, coffee plantations and tin and silver mines, as they were in danger of being occluded and marginalized totally from Malay or Malaysian political participation.

Interracial riots did occur in Malaysia but nowhere near the amount of bloodshed happened compared to the subsequent rioting that took place in comparable radically plural contexts British colonial contexts like Ceylon, Burma, or Bangladesh (much less also the Dutch of Indonesia.)

Thus we might conclude that the challenge faced mostly by the Babas and Nonyas, as members of a larger Peranakan and Overseas Chinese community was in essence transcultural and international, and was ultimately to retain a distinct but fundamentally core sense of Chinese identity in spite of and because of at times overwhelming patterns of assimilation, accommodation and amalgamation.

At any given time throughout the history of the Peranakan, until today in the post-Independence era of the nation-state of Malaysia, that the Peranakan Chinese identity would not be completely lost and washed away.

In this regard, therefore, the original Babas and Nonyas of the first Chinese-controlled Malacca faced the same essential dilemmas then as any of the 28 successive generations faced until even today.

That was to maintain a sense of distinct and respectable, trustworthy Chinese Peranakan identity vis-à-vis a larger and often terrible world, and to successfully reproduce their own world through successive future generations.

It is important to understand the parliamentary system of the Malay government, and the role of coalition, compromise and accommodation plays in maintaining a "balance of power" and underwriting the system of law and order represented by the reigning regime and Prime Minister of the Malaysian government.

Peranakan

Chinese style clan organization thrives in interstitial contexts, and filling marginal and peripheral positions intermediate between alternative and often competing or conflicting social structures provides opportunities (especially economic within broad interpretation) along with structural disadvantages (political and social counter-reference and marginalization.)

It is for these background factors that much is not well known or well preserved in terms of records of Peranakan and Baba Nonya activities. Much mystery will probably always surround that era.

Certainly, the original Chinese of *Bukit Cina* (or *Buket China*) in Malacca were a different set of lineages and situations under the Portuguese than under the Dutch a Century or two later, or then under the British another Century or two down the road.

Before closing this argument, I would suggest two basic problems to be considered. Eating of pork is a core part of the religion and daily cuisine of the Overseas Chinese, including presumably most Peranakan. But pork consumption by Muslims is not just haram, but fundamentally taboo, and the pig is seen as a dirty, polluting animal.

If passing as a Peranakan to permit intermarriage between Muslim and pork-loving Chinese religionists is possible, did this mean that either the Malay or Muslim wives of Chinese Towkays tolerated and lived with the consumption of pork within their households, or else had the Chinese husbands to give up this taste for pigs and confine themselves to halal types of food.

The other problem I have is to consider the Chinese question of normative relativity of the problem of "Face"—the transactionalism or reciprocal given and receiving of respect and respectability that has been so focal to Chinese cultural identity and normative ethos time immemorial.

Respectability Chinese style means trustworthiness, or that a person is trustworthy (within contexts of its situational interpretation, at least in appearances if not in actual terms.) Establishing face-to-face, interpersonal relationships of trust, even if at long distance or even if mediated through other, potentially a large number, of trustworthy or credible third parties.

How far would this style of Chinese social solidarity go before such a person is likely to have other ideas or second thoughts and choose an alternative course of action?

It strikes me that if the stereotypical Chinese is profit-minded supposedly always in his/her daily dealings with the larger world, this orientation is really the tip of an iceberg of the Chinese preoccupation with a sense of security and relative insecurity vis-à-vis a larger world, possibly born of the cyclical, periodic depravations to be expected in surviving and procreating in the traditional, changeless but always politically uncertain land of the Great Agrarian State.

One very knowledge mentor and advisor I had as a young graduate student told me that the Overseas Chinese were different from the mainland Chinese as what passed in Mainland China as a political preoccupation with a sense of security transposed itself overseas to a marked disinterest in local politics and instead a profound preoccupation with economic and social security.

In sociological research, it is understood that "the need for greater police protection" and predilection for authoritarian power structures, derives indirectly and unconsciously from a chronic background problem of economic uncertainty and insecurity—the role of a police person is to guard and protect the innocent civilian.

Whereas Americans would fear a thief stealing their belongings, a Chinese would fear more the possibility of their children being stolen somehow, whether by traffickers, malign spirits or misfortune.

In reported Peranakan birth practices, customary Chinese practices were followed that can only be interpreted as the extreme effort and preoccupation by the birth mother to protect and preserve the life of the young child at its most vulnerable.

The case of adoption and buying of babies by childless couples (where I was in Malaysia in the late 1980s, in the classified adds of the Straits Times, a female baby child cost something like $2-3,000.00 U.S., while a young baby boy cost about twice as much: $4-5,000, as my memory serves.)

These babies were presumably from poor and destitute families with too many children already, is one that presents itself as a viable option to many Overseas Chinese, especially with the assurance that such adoption would be clear and above board in terms of unquestioned parentage and custodial responsibilities. I can only imagine the go-between "baby estate" agent to be a fairly well off Chinese Dragon lady driving a fancy car.

The Socio-Structural Continuum of Straits Chinese Society

The center of Baba and Peranakan culture must be found somewhere along a continuum of possibilities between what it has meant to be traditionally Chinese, on one hand, and traditional Malay or other Indonesian on the other.

It must be found somewhere between being a sub-cultural and inter-ethnic orientation barely distinguishable in its basic components from the dominant cultures in which it was born and became situated, and being its own, fully grown Creole culture with its own distinctive orientation to the world.

It had its own basic patterning of cultural sanctions, views and values, and characteristics of personality that became enculturated and transmitted with each subsequent generation, and radically acculturated and amalgamated with each successive colonial era.

The terms "Peranakan," "Baba-Nonya," and "Straits Chinese" all have different sets of meanings, and are not completely synonymous with one another, though they all intersect and overlap considerably often in interest if sometimes confusing ways.

All three terms reflect one thing significant that they share, and that is the relative position of a core Chinese identity on a complex socio-cultural continuum in which there is assimilation, some acculturation, amalgamation and accommodation.

Yet the structure and identity of these people as traditionally Chinese was not washed away, or were their ancestral memories completely lost and forgotten in the shifting sands of time.

This diagram below does not include other creole cross-cultural groupings that arose and existed in these plural settings and descendants of whom still live and even in part carry on with distinctive ethno-cultural features and patterns.

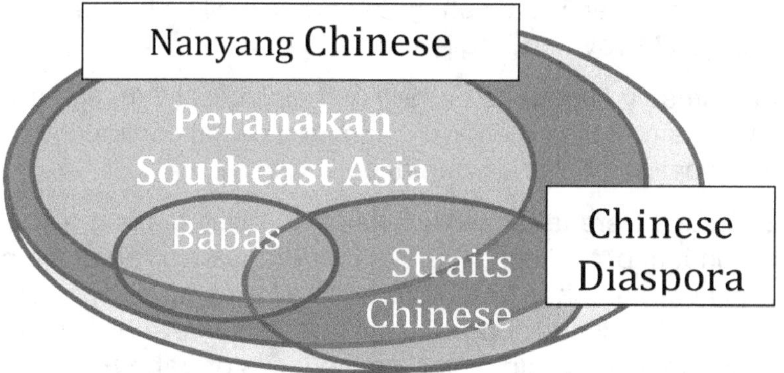

- The rules that are implied by this ordering are that "All Babas and Nonyas" are Peranakan but most Peranakan are not Babas and Nonyas.
- Most Babas are "Straits" Chinese but not all Chinese living in the Straits Settlements or in extension or outliers are necessarily Peranakan, nor especially

Baba/Nonya, even if they might be called "Chinese of the Straits Settlements."

- Where assimilation appears to have been high, as in Thailand and Burma, and possibly in Vietnam, there would have been overall a loss of identity and community structure within two or three generations, and a concomitant loss of clan-records, ancestral accounting and ritual ancestor worship practices.
- Where there remains some resistance and an intermediate location in that cross-cultural continuum, there remains a traditional ritualistic Chinese vertebra that has as part of the larger community body undergone some transformations of dress, speech, mannerisms, reference points and other appendages of the organic social body. Instead of clan books tracing back on.

There is another corresponding continuum of language in which the speech of the Babas and Peranakan lies along a continuum between spoken Amoy Hokkien, on one hand, and vernacular Malay, on the other, as well as between Chinese/Malay and English.

Presumably, language pattern and dialectical variation and stylistics reflected the larger Nanyang social continuum of historical and cultural adaptation.

Baba and Peranakan culture has also existed along a continuum of traditional versus modern, as well as along a continuum of urban versus rural. In all, we can distinguish these basic dimensions which intersect somewhere in the center that we would define as the locus of Baba/Peranakan culture.

If we can refer to the social construction of reality, in which processes of externalization, objectification, reification, subjectification and internalization are, in that order, dialectically interdependent and convergent in the critical moment of social reproduction and transmission, attendant especially upon the processes of primary and secondary socialization and discourse.

We can also talk about an antithetical "psychological reconstruction of reality" which, from an historical point of view, becomes somewhat independent and primary in the ongoing patterning and processes of cultural development and social history.

Once internalized in the form of such cognitive models, psycho-cultural orientations become in a sense "naturalized," habitualized, sub-conscious, and also, most importantly, self-fulfilling in rebounding back upon the social processes which led to their original constitution and constraint in the first place.

There is a sense in which ethos and ethnos represents an internalized frame of mind of the participant, and that though there is a wide range of divergence and variability between individuals, there is also some form of convergence upon common ground in core values, cognitive and normative orientations and collective symbolic representations upon which a consensus of shared ethnos is based.

To a great extent, a person's attitudes and outlook is a function of that person's social and structural position and situational context within this continuum, as well as a function of that person's capacity to negotiate and intermediate between alternative positions.

People commonly adopt and internalize status symbolisms which reflect not so much the reality of their status positioning within a society, but the ideal direction and expression of where that person ideally wants to be, as well as where that person may somewhat fictitiously believe him/herself to be.

But cognitive orientation and position also become dialectical in the articulation of social action and historical happenstance—to a large extent, given the appropriate circumstances such values and orientations do become 'self-fulfilling,' albeit in ways that most participants may not anticipate.

Furthermore, in entertaining the possibility of a variety of alternative positions within the cultural continuum, some of which may be mutually incompatible or contradictory, the ability to negotiate new positions and intermediate between them is a function of a person's past experience in doing so, as well as a function of that person's capacity to effectively mediate the boundaries between different positions, status-identities, roles, and internalized states of being.

Past experience with diversity results in an openness to new varieties of experience, whereas an "introverted" orientation to one or a few positions results in decreased capacity to integrate or deal effectively with a wide range of plurality.

Furthermore, the ability to negotiate boundaries demands the mastery of certain social skills—the ability to linguistically, emotively, cognitively and behaviorally code-switch and code-mix; the ability to function along a number of parallel continuums of cognitive orientation, and to adopt the "other's" point of view.

In this sense we must see psycho-cultural identity as a function of a kind of "cognitive pluralism" in which an individual is able to maintain a number of different cognitive orientations in relation to one another within a single universe of experience, and we may properly refer to an "ethno-psychology" of social experience.

There is a suggestion for a weak form of the linguistic relativity hypothesis in that code-switching between Malay, English and Hokkien requires the adoption of different conceptual codes and cognitive orientations which have different foci, different dimensions of significance and salience, and which exclude some elements that are central in other cognitive orientations.

Though the basic cognitive structure may remain the same in each of the cases, the "cognitive style" of orientation and operation between orientations may be quite different, and even contradictory.

Furthermore, the internalization of code-switching/mixing in complex social situations to accommodate for diversity acquires a mode of social functioning that becomes habitual and automatic, based on a wide latitude of "native speaker/hearer intuition" which must not only fill in the many gaps, but cross-over the many switching points.

There is in this sense that such a complex, heterogeneous orientation, is based upon a kind of minimal structure, like a pidgin or creole, which is in many of its features reduced in the amount of constraint or redundancy it requires.

Code-switching/mixing discourse must have a structure that is open to many variables and quite flexible in its applicability.

And what is true on a linguistic level is reflective and representative of a deeper symbolic and culturally encoded level of cognition and experience—people are not only switching and mixing codes in a quasi-regular but informal way on a linguistic level, but also upon meta-linguistic and cultural levels as well.

Language, religious orientation in both values and world-view, and ethnic identity are all interrelated in certain important ways.

Language comes to reflect our symbolic universe of understanding, and our language becomes a primary vehicle for the expression and realization of such symbolic understanding.

Who we are and what we are become defined by the words we use, and the words we use become framed within the compass of our social knowledge and the kind of social understandings with which we approach the world.

Ethnicity and ethnic consciousness are a kind of relative psychosocial identity that falls somewhere within the dialectic between the spoken and textual realities of the language we use, and the social and symbolic contexts of relation in which we use that language.

The problematic understanding of Ethnoculture comes to rest upon the nexus of relations between language, religious beliefs and values, and ethnic identity. Language has a tremendous internal consistency and order. It has its own separate sense of history, change and directionality of development.

Religious orientation is also a kind of living, performed symbolic system. It has a traditional momentum that, through processes of socialization, shape and reshape human character and culture in a constraining and conservative way.

Ethnicity, and ethnic stereotypes, reemerges time and again with amazing persistence in spite of the social processes and historical forces that always threaten to disintegrate them, despite ideological prejudices that seek always to deny them, stigmatize or euphemize them, or even efface or eradicate them.

To summarize, Overseas Chinese social structure of the Straits Settlements provided an extremely adaptable form of clan based social organization that allowed for the realization and development of a distinctive but largely interstitial Peranakan Straits Chinese society. These clans and their interconnected associations, many of which were secret, permitted among other possibilities the rapid mobilization of up to a hundred or more men at one place and time to meet immediate emergency conditions. These groups could form and even more rapidly disappear back into the woodwork of traditional Nanyang society. These clans provided their members a means of making a living and meaning to their world; mechanisms for labor and trade/craft specialization, networks for resource acquisition and bartering, and a means for developing a larger world more suitable to their interests.

VI: The Places of the Peranakan

"Peranakan" is more or less specific in reference where the predominant lingua franca to be found will be some dialectical version of Bahasa (Malay language). In general significance it also indirectly refers to a much broader range of people and places that ultimately reached across the entire region of Southeast Asia, even reaching into places of the Pacific Island regions, as well as into the South Asian region, and possibly even further to East Africa or the coastal areas of the Middle East.

We find similar varieties of Peranakan-like people in the Kalimantan and Sabah, Sarawak, Brunei, the Philippines, in Vietnam, in Cambodia, in Thailand, in Burma, and possibly in Laos. To what degree, and in what way, Chinese populations become thus creolized without losing basic features of their Chinese cultural heritage and sense of civilization remains probably yet a largely unexplored and understudied topic yet, though the highly suggestive evidence abounds almost anywhere one looks across these places.

Sense of place, like sense of period, are thus very important to the distinguishing of unique Peranakan identity vis-à-vis the modern nation-states they occupy, their history and patterns of settlement and making a living, and their patterns of assimilation and relative acculturation or amalgamation.

Mestizo Chinese

The formation of the Baba culture may have been unique in Southeast Asian History, but cultural correlates are to be found in other places and other periods of the Nanyang. The mestizo Chinese of the Philippines, distinguishable there since the eighteenth century, have made important contributions to the historical development of the Philippines, being mainly implicated in the Philippine Revolution against the Spanish, serving as a major catalyst in social change and economic development of the Philippines, and constituting a leading component in Hispanicization and creation of a distinctive Filipino culture.

Structurally similar to the Babas, they represented a pariah group situated between the ethnically stronger Chinese and the indigenous Filipinos. ".... In most parts of Southeast Asia the Chinese mestizos (to use the Philippine term for persons of mixed Chinese-native ancestry) have not been formally or legally recognized as a separate group—one whose membership is strictly defined by genealogical considerations rather than by place of birth, and one which, by its possession of a unique combination of cultural characteristics, could be easily distinguished from both the Chinese and native communities."(E. Wickberg, "The Chinese Mestizo in Philippine History", in Journal of Southeast Asian History, Vol. 5, no 1, 1964)

These Chinese mestizos had become prominent in landholding, wholesale merchant activities, and in the professions. They grew in wealth as a middleman pariah class, concentrating and virtually monopolizing on the internal trade of the Philippines.

The Chinese mestizos of the Philippines were strongly Hispanicized: politically, in the adoption of Catholicism, and in the adoption of Philippine versions of Hispanic culture. Their dress was unique in this regard—"models of what the urbanized Filipino of the late nineteenth century would wear." (Ibid, pg. 1964)

Their culture was urbanized, and the maternal influence Hispanicized, Catholicized mothers in the rearing and socialization of the children, were important factors in the development of the cultural distinctiveness of the Chinese mestizo.

Métis Chinois'

The Chinese presence in Cambodia and Cochin China, or what later became South Vietnam, has been very old. Early evidence from the Eleventh and Twelfth Centuries A.D. mention the presence of a small Chinese community in Anghor Thom, merchants and carpenters who came by sea and who married local women.

By the Thirteenth Century, a substantial Chinese settlement in Phnom-Penh is noted, and the emergence of this center from a locally oriented one to a major foreign trade entrepôt, coincides with this settlement. The Portuguese found Chinese communities there by the Spanish, and later, during the Sixteenth and Seventeenth centuries. Cantonese mercenaries in the service of the Annamese emperor established a fort at *Mytho* along the Mekong.

After more than a century of occupation, these Chinese were later forced to abandon this settlement and migrated to the location near Saigon that later became known as Cholon.

"...And soon established a trading town that soon became the centre of Chinese trade for the whole of Indochina. Many of these Chinese adventurers married Annamese women and produced the *Minh-Huong*, the Sino-Annamese who were treated as a separate minority group throughout the nineteenth century in Annam and Cochin China, and who, for a short period, constituted a separate legal group in Cambodia as well." (W. E. Willmott, "History and Sociology of the Chinese in Cambodia Prior to the

French Protectorate," in <u>The Journal of Southeast Asian History, Vol. 7</u>, no. 1, 1966)

By the time of the arrival of French and British explorers, Phnom-Penh was mostly a Chinese city, composed primarily of immigrants from Cholon, and who had tied up the local trade in fish and rice. These Chinese were probably mostly Cantonese and Hainanese, the descendants of Ming patriots.

Reference is made in the legal code of the Khmer Kingdom to granting of positions of authority over the Chinese community to "Me'tis-Chinois." (Lecle're, 1898:115) Chinese were not subject to the legal marriage prohibitions between Cambodian Buddhists and foreigners—perhaps because they were Buddhist as well, and because it was relatively easy for a Chinese to assimilate, if he so desired, into Cambodian society. "Any Chinese born in Cambodia was considered a Cambodian if he adopted Khmer customs and dress. Sino-Khmer were automatically Cambodians." (Ibid, pg. 31)

Thai (Siamese)-Chinese

The Chinese in Thailand represent another instance of partial assimilation and the formation of an important pariah group. Constituting perhaps an eighth of the total population, they are small traders and merchant middlemen—"virtually any article bought or sold in Thailand passes through the hands of one or more Chinese middlemen." (Richard Coughlin, <u>Double-Identity</u> 1960: 2)

Chinese traders in Thailand date back at least to the Thirteenth Century. A French account from 1687 reports about 3,000 Chinese at *Ayuthia*. By this time, the Chinese controlled most of the trade in the country.

Teochiu Chinese, Taksin, rose to power as the King of Siam after expelling Burmese invaders who had destroyed the capital. The predominant presence of Teochiu Chinese in Thailand is probably related to this important historical episode. His son-in-law, Chao Phya Chakkri, who founded the present Bangkok Dynasty, assassinated Taksin. The royal palace was established in the old Chinese quarter of the city, "ruled by a rich Chinese merchant with the noble rank of Phraya."

Continual warfare with Burma and Cambodia had decimated the Thai population, and thus Chinese immigration was welcome. "Meanwhile a war-surplus of females became available to the bachelor (or otherwise) Chinese immigrants and Chinese blood was literally fused with both the royal and common blood of the Thai people." (Joseph P. L. Jiang, "The Chinese in Thailand: Past and Present", in The Journal of Southeast Asian History, Vol. 7, no. 1, 1966:42)

Chinese figured prominently in the economic development of Thailand—they held many "tax-farms" and controlled the junk trade that was held by a royal monopoly on foreign commerce. They constituted artisans, craftsmen, metal smiths, and builders, as well as engaging in mining, planting and timber.

Chinese-Thai intermarriage was great in old Siam, and there seems to have been no boundaries or discrimination against such amalgamation. The net effect seems to have been near complete assimilation of Chinese by the third or fourth generation, with only some Chinese cultural elements, such as ancestor worship, remaining. "Since the earliest times prominent Chinese were often recruited to governmental, especially diplomatic service. The majority of these were second generation, and were more than half assimilated..." (Jiang, 1966: pg. 51)

Peranakan

The status of the Nanyang Chinese in Thailand was directly tied to Thai tributary tutelage to Mainland China, and to their usefulness to both the Thai royalty and to the Thai people in economic activities. The Chinese were not discriminated against, and were given virtually free and ungoverned reign in their own spheres of activity, and yet the Chinese were clearly made politically subordinate to the Royalty.

They filled a critical, intermediary niche as a pariah group which was not traditionally a part of Thai social structure, but which was necessary and vital to the economic development of old Siam.

With the encroachment of Western domination over China, the Chinese loss of status to the Thai Royalty signaled a reversal in the status of the Chinese in Thailand, so much so that by the early 20th Century we find mention of the Chinese of Thailand as "Asian Jewry" and the promotion of Thai nationalism, an orientation inherited from the West, is closely linked to growing anti-Sinicism. Policies of enforced assimilation of the ethnic Chinese into Thai culture—"Thaification"—and of systematic discrimination against the Chinese in business and public life have grown and continue unabated until today.

Burmese-Chinese

The Chinese in Burma are not outstanding in the History of the Nanyang. Burma shares a common border with Mainland China, and this has constrained status of the Overseas Chinese there in important ways that the Chinese of Burma have not been ignorant in taking advantage.

Though highly visible in many sectors of the economy, they were never as economically predominant there as elsewhere in Southeast Asia, in part because they had close competition with Indian merchants.

Victor Purcell notes that intermarriage between Chinese men and Burmese women was not uncommon, and that the male offspring of such unions remained identified as Chinese, while the female offspring became identified as Burmese.

He goes on to remark that Chinese there become almost completely assimilated by the second or third generation, losing all their Chinese-ness—thus, despite a continual influx of new Chinese immigrants into Burma, the total number of people identified as Chinese there remains effectively stable.

"Borneo" Chinese

Evidence supports the possible presence of Chinese upon the island of Borneo from as early as the 7th Century, and possibly even earlier, with archaeological evidence dating to 117 BC, upon an old site in the region now occupied by Brunei and Sarawak. (Victor Purcell, 1966:11)

Early Chinese Chronicles of the Liang (502-566) and Sui (589-618) Dynasties mention "*P'oli*," known since the Tang (618-907) Dynasty onwards as "*P'oni*" and thought to be the early name for Brunei, had given a description of its direction and of it's inhabitants which fit well that of Borneo. Later Chronicles mention the same kingdom comprising fourteen provinces extending along the northern Borneo coastline and as far as the Philippines. (John Chin, <u>The Sarawak Chinese</u> 1981:1-2)

Assimilation of Chinese, as ulu-traders, in Borneo, is held to have been widespread. Rates of intermarriage with native *Dusun* and *Sulu* peoples were probably high. The Chinese have long figured in the "*ulu*" trade and resource exploitation of Borneo, as well as in its mining and agricultural pioneering.

An early Kong Si system provided the organizational base for the mobilization of labor and resources in the development of trade and resource production in Borneo. Trade networks with indigenous peoples brought them into continuous contacts and interactions with these peoples, as these people grew accustomed to their goods and their presence.

Chinese now comprise a significant minority in Borneo, comprising most of the ethnic-dialect groups representing the Overseas Chinese. Intermarriage with local wives was frequent, especially in the earlier periods, in part because of the male-biased sex ratio among the Chinese, and because such conjugal unions facilitated economic relations with the indigenous peoples.

More recently, such intermarriage is virtually nonexistent, in either urban or rural segments of Chinese society, and "Peranakan" of means are remarrying back into "pure" Chinese society. "When it does occur it reflects the low status of the individual involved and his difficulty in finding an acceptable mate within the bounds of his own ethnic group." (David Fortier, "The Chinese in North Borneo," 1957:16-7)

The Period of the Peranakan People

The Peranakan people have been time-travelers, especially in the modern era to the extent that they maintain some memory and celebration of their heritage, manners and customs and culture, at least in reenactment if not the actual living or revitalization of that former world.

We do not have a good and deep history of the Peranakan people, and their proto-history shades rapidly into archaeological prehistory. Evidence suggests that Chinese were directly or indirectly interacting on the Island of Borneo for at least a couple of thousand years.

We do not have to reference Admiral Cheng Ho of the Ming Dynasty for the baseline of the Overseas Chinese settlements (aka Malacca) which settlement was soon eclipsed by the arrival of the Portuguese. Chinese were probably sending out trading expeditions and possible exploratory fleets or fishing expeditions into these regions for hundreds of years prior to European colonization.

The Chinese migration and peopling of Southeast Asia may have been nothing more or less than the Maritime extension of the "March South" of Chinese populations, blocked eventually at the Red River in Northern Vietnam, and channeling around and down by sea, stream, coast, and inland passages.

There has been nothing new or little now outdated about people, caught between a rock of poverty and a hard spot of political repression, taking to boats to escape to a hopeful paradise, or at least some foreign shore free of their previous tyrannies.

This pattern of migration, and exodus, has been happening throughout the human past time-immemorial and there is no reason to believe that it wasn't the same particularly in a maritime and crossroads region that Southeast Asia has always been.

There is no gain saying today whether the culture of the Proto-Peranakan people say of the 15th-16th Centuries was the same or even similar to the cultures of the Straits Chinese as this developed during the 18th and early 19th Century. While we might be surprised by some of the transformational differences found in different periods, we might become even more surprised by the continuities that tradition and religion helped to conserve through many generations.

VII: Marriage Customs

Baba and Nonya customs of marriage are in some respects unique, and have both Malay and Chinese elements incorporated into an elaborate ritual ceremony. This ceremony, as well as the institution of marriage among the Babas, has been a central topic in the discourse about their cultural uniqueness.

Chinese marriage practices are dominant. Both newlyweds are adorned with traditional Chinese marriage costumes. Matchmaking was Malay in style, except for the exchange of horoscopes, which was traditionally Chinese. The "*lap-chai*" ceremony was held three days before the wedding. The groom's family would send twelve attendants bearing gifts to the bride's family's home, or "*rumpah abu,*" to the accompaniment of Chinese trumpets.

These presents were carried on brass or red lacquered trays, and were all of Malay origin or which bore Malay names—"*kian songket*" (embroidered sarong), "*belanja kalwin*" (marriage expenses). These included several "ang pows" or red packets of money, the first "*wang tetok*" containing 12 dollars and called "nursing money," the second called "*wang belinja*" and called "expense allowance" and a third called "*wang sireh*" or "betel nut money", and "*pinang mas*" (golden betel nuts) and "*pisang rajah*" or "a comb of a species of bananas known as "royal bananas." (Ho Wing Meng, 1976: 31).

There is also a tray containing the marriage agreement called "*surat kahwin,*" written in Chinese characters. The bridegroom's attendant, the "*Pak chindek*" was dressed in

Malay costume. Otherwise, there were no striking differences in marriage customs from those of the Hokkien Chinese.

My wife mentions that in the wedding ceremonies of very wealthy Nonyas, Indian servants would be hired to carry large trays of the bride wealth along the streets, and that this was a big occasion attended by many spectators. The payment of bride price included a sum of money, or "*pien kim*," which ranged in the mid-Nineteenth Century from 60 to 100 dollars.

> "Business was frequently brought to a stop in Penang while traders and others craned their necks from upper windows to see the procession of a wedded couple's gifts." On large and nicely decorated carts were placed furniture, washstands, plates, other household utensils, jewelry, and so forth. Behind and in front marched the musicians, in all kinds of uniform with a variety of instruments, principal among tem being the ubiquitous drum..." (John Balibain, Hail Penang! 1932: pg. 131)

For a complete description of a traditional Peranakan wedding, the reader is referred to the excellent account by Ruth Ho; (Rainbow Round My Shoulder, 1975: pgs. 6-28), and, somewhat surprisingly, by J. D. Vaughn; (The Manners and Customs of the Chinese of the Straits Settlements, 1879: pgs. 22-29)

The more modern Babas and Peranakan have dropped many of the paraphernalia, and costs, of such elaborate wedding rituals. They have often adopted western style wedding dress, which can be seen in many wedding photos.

Tan Giok-lan (1963) writes: "One of the most radical changes that occurred was the discarding of the elaborate and heavy traditional Chinese robes; they were exchanged for the western white dress and veil for the bride and the dark or light suit for the groom."

"The wearing of western apparel was already taking place around 1920. The writer was informed that the last time a bridal couple was dressed in traditional Chinese style in *Sukabumi* was around 1930, but this was only for the ceremony; thereafter they put on western-style dress." (Tan Giok Lan, 1963: pg. 86)

Tan goes on to note that wedding ceremony is one of the best examples of the incorporation of elements from all three cultural backgrounds—there are apparently no rigid rules and no strong consensus about correctness.

A wide range of selection is possible, and no social criticism is attached to such selection. Selection of wedding elements tends to follow the amount of modernization, Westernization, or Chineseness or Indonesian acculturation of the newly weds and their families.

"There is one ritual, however, which is never omitted, except in families converted to Christianity. This is the honoring of the groom's ancestors by both the bride and groom, which is essentially the traditional Chinese ceremony of presentation of the bride to the groom's ancestors, thereby incorporating her in his lineage." (Tan, 1963: pg. 87)

Matrilocality is a typically and distinctively Baba cultural trait that is noted by many authors. The husband of the newlywed usually goes to live in the home of the bride.

This is a rather uncommon pattern among more traditional Chinese that became more prevalent among the Straits Chinese and which deserves some explanation.

Surname exogamy, except for marriage between kin of different ranks, and tolerance of marriage between maternal first cousins were all Chinese practices that were in general carried on by the traditional Babas, but not as strictly adhered to.

Matrilocality also sometimes became uxorilocality and matriarchy, especially when the bride's lineage had no agnatic issue and thus depended upon bringing in a son-in-law to adopt the paternal surname of the bride.

This type of matrilocal marriage was not an unknown practice among the more traditional Chinese. "But among the latter it is regarded shameful for a man to enter into such a marriage as in Hokkien colloquial he is said to 'sell his lantern' (*Boe toa-teng*) and in *Tiechiu* to 'have his ribs trampled upon' (*thiam phian-li*)." (Maurice Freedman, 1962)

Freedman in fact referred to such a kind of husband as "as sort of male daughter-in-law." A more common form of matrilocal marriage was *chin-tsin*, in which a man on being married lived in his wife's home without prejudice to his rights as a father." (Png Poh-Seng; pg. 112)

Freedman notes that the practice of uxorilocality had persisted until recent times. The children of such marriages take the father's surname and inherit property from him, but "are raised mainly among their matrilateral kin (people related to them on their mother's side) and in houses that tend to pass down the generations through women.

My wife's sister's husband, whose family came from Singapore, and who did not have money, moved into the Nonya mother's household in Penang, the mother having paid for all the wedding arrangements as well as the bride-wealth.

Peranakan

The mother helped the children, and the grandchildren, financially as well as caretaking, and treated the son-in-law quite well. The husband stayed with the household until the mother broke up with the father.

Birth Customs

Nonya women were strict adherents of traditional Chinese customs and beliefs relating to childbirth. They observed taboos relating to the killing of animals, moving furniture in the home, digging gardens or repairs, "for fear that the baby might be born with disfiguring marks" (Png Poh-Seng, 1969:pg. 114).

Women who had given birth were ritually confined for a month, and those who visited her risked "contamination." Medicinal foods were given during this time for the healing of the mother.

At one month, food is given out, including *nasi kyunit*, curry chicken, red eggs, Chinese *koay*—the rice and curry are customs that other Chinese seem to have picked up from the Nonyas.

Among the Peranakan of Sukabumi, Tan Giok-Lan (1963: pg. 88) noted that the ideal of patrilocality is strictly observed, except upon numerous occasions in which availability of accommodations or lack of money mitigate the arrangements.

It is interesting that in Ruth Ho's account of the wedding ceremonies, that if during the ceremony the bride managed to step on the bridegroom's toes, "it meant that she would be the more aggressive partner. It seems that some brides' mothers made it a point to tell their daughters to be sure to step on HIS toes!" (Ho, 1975: pg. 20)

She also notes that throughout the Peranakan wedding, "one is struck most forcibly not only by the dependence on astrology, symbolism or what some people might call plain superstition, but also by the great importance attached to virtue, filial piety, respect for elders and familial ties..." (Ho, 1975: pg. 26)

G. Minchin, in another classic description of the Peranakan wedding (Notes and Queries on China and Japan, Vol. 4, no. 6, 1870, pg. 85), writes: "It is a strange fact, that when any real Chinaman is married in Malacca or Singapore, he is obliged to talk Malay to his wife in order to be understood."

VIII: Baba Religion

Religious orientation has always been an important factor in the Southeast Asian setting, especially to the extent that religion becomes implicated in the mediation of cultural and ethnic boundaries. "Religion is one of the main mechanisms that defines and maintains ethnic boundaries in Southeast Asian societies." (John Clammer, 1980: 45)

The negativity of the boundary to intermarriage and cultural assimilation that Islam has maintained, the fundamental incompatibility with basic Islamic values and Buddhist values, as well as basic differences between a Muslim cultural orientation and a traditional Chinese one, have all been pointed out as contributing to the maintenance of a separate Peranakan community. In this regard, religious conversion can be a mechanism of assimilation, just as religious orthodoxy can be a mechanism of boundary-maintenance.

A survey conducted in Malacca in 1976 (John Clammer, 1980) revealed that 70 percent of the Babas professed faith in the traditional Chinese Religious orientation. Twenty percent comprised a "no-religion/free thinker" category; eight percent were nominally Christian, and the remaining two-percent "being members of minority religious movements." There were no Muslims. Of course, people who would have professed their faith in Islam would probably have become fully incorporated into the Malay community.

One basic difference between the Peranakan communities of Java and the Baba communities of the Straits Settlements was the number of the former who were Muslim, in part constituting the basis of their Peranakan identity. In L.A.P. Gosling's study of the assimilation and migration of rural

Chinese of Terengganu (a northeastern mostly rural province of Malaya), movement by Baba Chinese into the Malay community posed no real problem, as outwardly they were already very assimilated, genetically they were mixed.

Of course, Islam is diverse and broad in practice. Indonesia was never the monolithic source of traditional Islamic identity as it became in Malaysia after independence. In Malaysia, political identity is fused with religious identity. Indonesia, de facto Islamic, never need to assert its fundamentalism of Islamic religious authority over the entire nation state composed of significant minorities of other religions.

Because of their general social positioning at an attenuated and tenuous distance from their own Chinese cultural tradition, the geniality and general acceptance of the Baba's by the Malays, the rather simple process of conversion by profession of faith, the relaxed and secure pace of life among the Malays, all contributed to the pull of Peranakan into the mainstream of the host society. "The major element in the loss of population was the increased assimilation of Babas into the Malay community."

Rates of assimilation vary between different religious communities vary—it is greater between Chinese and Christian, Hindu and especially for Theravada Buddhists, than it has been between Chinese and Muslims, or between any of the other faiths and Islam.

Perhaps the most important difference is that in order for a Muslim to marry a person who is non-Muslim, then that partner must convert to the faith, even if only nominally. This alone creates a barrier around Islam such as does not exist for other religions.

In this regard must also be noted the great degree of mutual tolerance, even respect, for the deities, temples and ritual practices of people of different faiths within the plural societies of Southeast Asia. People may be nominally one faith or another, and regularly attend its ceremonies, and yet also frequently pay homage or attend ceremonies of other faiths.

From a Chinese standpoint all religions are non-exclusive and a practitioner's standpoint have some measure or modicum of credible spiritual and symbolic efficacy.

The degree of religious syncretism commonly found in Southeast Asia is unusual in the World. In such religiously plural contexts, religiosity, holiness, spirituality and sacredness are common values recognized in the deities, icons, beliefs, and ritual practices of many different faiths. A local spirit, a *kramat*, or whether a deity that is in origin Hindu or Theravada Buddhist or Mahayana Buddhist or Taoist, is given the same degree of passing respect as any other.

The prevalence of new religious movements and minority religious cults, and their popularity in Malaysia, is another indication of the basically syncretic religious orientation to be found there. The only exception to this rule is the Mosque, which remains effectively closed off to outsiders' participation or visitation. "Islam.... Has two leading characteristics which contrast with this—it is exclusive (as opposed to syncretic and eclectic), and it is closely tied to a particular social structure, so much so that in Malaysia the idea of a non-Muslim Malay is quite unthinkable." (John Clammer, 1980:47)

Evidence of this syncretic orientation among the Peranakan is also available—part of what it means to become a good Malay and a good Moslem is in a sense to accept only one God and to close the doors of one's imagination and curiosity about other possibilities.

Traditional Chinese religious orientation can be defined by the "Conflation of the Three Teachings." Tan Giok-Lan, in her ethnography of the Peranakan Sukabumi, (1963) records an important Peranakan religious organization —"*Sam Kauw Hee*"—one which is predominantly composed of Peranakan Chinese families.

"*Sam Kauw*" means literally "Three Religions"—referring to Buddhism, Confucianism and Taoism. This organization was oriented towards the promotion of traditional Chinese religious values. (Tan Giok-Lan, 1963:158) A strong syncretic religious movement in Singapore, one of many organizations there, was called the "Red Swastika Society."

Baba religious orientation shares with other Chinese religious orientations its tolerance and syncretism, often under the same roof, of many, competing, often Non-Chinese religious orientations. Babas observe, but in general do not adhere as strictly to, the Chinese festival calendar, and they also regularly participate in other traditional magico-religious systems, such as temple worship, ancestor worship, consultation of the Chinese horoscope, geomancy, etc.

They have also adopted a number of more indigenous Malay magico-religious beliefs and customs—worship of *kramats* or local deities, *Dato Kramats*, or spirit-mediums, consultation of Malay *bomohs*, or traditional medical practitioners, use of magical charms, etc. Malay elements, such as the offering of satay, sireh or lime, are also incorporated into Chinese religious rituals.

The first Chinese temple built in Malaya was the *Cheng Hoon Teng* Temple in *Bukit Cina* in Malacca. In 1704 Chan Li Lock built the main hall of the temple and placed there the figure of the Goddess of Mercy, or "Kwan yin" or "*padma-pani.*" (Yeh Jen Fen, Historical Guide to Malacca, pg. 81-2)

Peranakan

The preeminence of the Goddess of Mercy in the Straits
Settlements is important to a consideration of early Chinese
religion in Malaysia. J. D. Vaughn details the design of the
Goddess of Mercy Temple in Pitt St. in Penang, which dates
to 1848, still the main and most active temple of worship by
the Chinese in Penang. We had offering made during our
wedding day there by my wife's God Mom, her old Amah who
cared for her when she was a child.

Victor Purcell, in his work <u>The Chinese in Malaya</u>, gave a
long account of the origin of Kwan Yin as "one of the most
popular goddesses in the Chinese pantheon. "

The Chinese of the Straits must not be mistaken as taking
their religion lightly or not seriously—the pragmatism of their
religious devotions has fundamental spiritual, moral and
utilitarian efficacy that is taken quite seriously by the
Chinese.

In an uncertain world, conversion to Christianity has been
increasingly seen as a viable option for many Straits
Chinese. Conversion to Christianity actually "promotes
interethnic marriage or inter-communal marriage, in the
former case between Chinese and Eurasian, and in latter
case between Baba and non-Baba." (John Clammer, 1980:
pg. 55)

The religious component is separate from other components
of language, culture, and race in the ethno-cultural identity of
the Chinese. Among the Malay, being Muslim is central to
that identity."...The religious factor, far from being a
peripheral one, is actually central to the study of the
assimilation, integration or lack of assimilation of Chinese
minorities to their "host cultures" throughout Southeast Asia.
(Clammer, 1980: pg.59)

Another aspect of religious syncretism notable among the Peranakan are particular beliefs, ritual-religious practices and ceremonies. A striking example is the use of water with flower petals and cut lime as a purifying or cleansing agent. A friend wanted to give us this ceremony while in Malaysia because of a small streak of misfortunes we had been having.

My wife gave me a variant of the same bath during a later period in which we were having a run of hard times. She mixed the flower petals from seven different kinds of flowers, and cut half a lime, and poured the water over my head three times.

"The client or the person on whose behalf the client sought the spirit medium's help, has to have a bath including a hair wash before taking a ritual bath. The lime is squeezed and the juice is then poured over the body of the person. The spirit medium stresses that the pulp of the lime must be thrown away after the ritual bath." (Cecilia Ng Siew Hua, "The Sam Poh Neo Neo Keramat: A Study of a Baba Chinese Temple", 1983: pg. 118)

"Ritual baths with water only are a common part of Malay animism—water is interpreted as a 'boundary weakener,' which, therefore allows passage from one state to another." (J. Endicott, 1970)

The Chinese believe that the lime, petal and water concoction clean impurities from the body. Lime is seen also as a cleansing agent—the impurities becoming concentrated in the lime pulp. Lime is also used for divination by a spirit-medium in trance.

In this case, seven lime pieces are cut, just as the petals of seven flowers are used—seven "transcends distinctions based on differences in colour" (Endicott, 1970:pg. 137) It too, becomes a boundary weakener. "Though the Malays seem to have no unified symbolic classification based on colour, differences of colours are often used to establish or indicate particular boundaries between significant categories." (Ibid. pg. 137)

Cecilia Ng, in her analysis of the practices of a Baba temple, notes that the spirit deities of the temple are "ethnically ambiguous" which parallels the ethnic ambiguity of the Baba Chinese. "The consultation, however, is conducted in both the ways of the Malay Animist and the Chinese Religionist; ritual paraphernalia limes, petals and benzoin are often used in Malay animism while the red dye, charm papers and the seal of the deities are characteristic of Chinese Religion.

The Peranakan have accepted the "keramats" who "can be either people, animals or inanimate things which have supernatural powers," (1983: pg. 124) but in the case of this particular study they are not inclined to seek the services of "*bomohs*" or healers, "who they perceive to be evil sorcerers conjuring spells and creating trouble." (Ibid. pg. 124) Ng compares her study of the Baba temple with an earlier study, the only of its kind, by Rosie Tan of a spirit medium who was probably a Peranakan and who served the Baba community.

Rosie Tan's study (1958) deals with "*kramats*" as local shrines dedicated to honored spirit deities, marking often the graves of local holy men or founding fathers, and the more popular of which attract a great many pilgrims and supplicants.

Private "*kramats*" do not have a "*Datu Kramat*" and therefore require a spirit medium to call upon and intercede with the spirits on behalf of the worshippers. Worshippers beseech the advice and aid of the *Datu Kramats* for a variety of reasons—for husbands, for children, for health, or for information.

Ng concludes her study by stating that while the *Datuk Shaik Ismail* shrine had more overt Malay elements, the *Sam Poh Neo Neo* temple was Chinese religionist at the structural level, at the periphery of the Chinese religious system, with many borrowings from Malay animism. "The religious system under study is not syncretic, but borrows certain elements from Malay Animism and incorporates these into an essentially Chinese religious system."(Ng. 1983: pg.129)

The Baba's choose Malay rather than Chinese religious elements, because the important reference group against which they must distinguish themselves is not the Malay, but the Chinese. "It is therefore logical that Malay elements were used as emblems to accentuate their differences from the ethnic Chinese." (Ibid. pg. 129)

The earlier study of the more Malay shrine differed from the later example of the *Sam Poh Neo Neo* temple because "the Baba Chinese no longer enjoy the favoured position of social brokers and indeed with the multi-racial ideology which was widely publicized in recent years, the Baba Chinese are faced with either not fitting into the publicly accepted model of society or alternatively to redefine their ethnic boundaries and identify themselves with the Chinese." (Ibid. Pg. 129)

The fact that the Babas of the temple "*bai*" (pray to) all the deities as if of the same "Chinese" pantheon is not convincing counter-evidence against the thesis of the inherent syncretism of Chinese religious orientation. In fact if anything, it is a demonstration of just such syncretism that the Chinese would treat all deities as if their own.

> "It would appear that these Malay elements are but emblems to distinguish the ethnic Baba Chinese; from the ethnic Chinese.... In more general terms it can be said that a section of the Baba Chinese population

practice a religion that is the religion of many Chinese in Singapore." (Ibid.130)

While living in Penang, I attended with my wife and her friends a "Birthday Party" for a local Malay deity. The party went for three days straight and was attended by numerous Chinese, many of who were quite respectable and well off. The spirit medium was a Chinese man dressed in the outfit of a Malay bomoh. It was conducted in a Chinese home in which the Shrine had been erected. The Birthday was given for the benefit of children who had been born with handicaps. Many Chinese attended and gave offerings of donations in exchange for talismans.

Food was served freely—*nasi kunyit,* chicken curry, *and bee hoon.* No pork was served—the food was cooked in brand new pots and pans for purity. The *Datuk* smoked "*Cheerot*" a heavy Malay cigar, and went into a trance, danced the "*ronggeng*" with Malay dancing girls as well as with Chinese.

There was a Malay band. He performed "automatic writing" on the ground—giving numbers which people kept note of what he would mark upon the ground—the number spreading through the crowd like wildfire.

An older Chinese matron went into a trance and began dancing—becoming the focal point for the audience. The show would last from evening until 12:00. In the morning there were prayer sessions that people would randomly visit. Not all of these people were Peranakan—many were very traditionally Chinese, yet the indigenous Malay elements, the structure of the whole ceremony, and the syncretism of the event, its spiritual importance for a larger urban community, could not be ignored.

Tan Chee Beng, in his account of the Peranakan Chinese from the same area (1982), describes the same kind of celebration, but as a Hokkien ceremony, which, like with the Penang Hokkien, refer to the ceremony as "Ang Kong su;" or "The Affairs of the Deities." The patron god of the local town has no temple, but is taken care of by different families in rotation.

The ceremony takes place in the compound of the home that holds the altar. Each year divination is employed to select a committee to take care of the Deities altar.

"The celebration usually lasts for three or four days...Part of the celebration involves a spirit-medium going into trance. In the evening, *menora* drama is staged. This is a kind of Thai dance-drama in which songs are presented in Kelantan Thai but comic verses are usually presented in Kelantan Malay...."(Ibid. pg. 42)

The *menora*, or "*Nora Chatri*," is a local Thai-Malay folk dance form that derived from the *Sudhana-Manohra* tale of the *Jatakas*. Its features and associated beliefs are strongly linked to animistic and shamanistic orientations "upon which the *Sudhana-Manohara*" story has been planted."(Ghulam-Sarwar Yousof, "Nora Chatri in Kedah: A Preliminary Report," JMBRAS Vol. 55, no. 1, 1982: pg. 53)

The dance lasts for three consecutive nights, and is performed for ritual occasions as well as for entertainment.

Part of the performance involves an opening trance session in which performers and non-performers participate to the rhythms of the Gamelan music that slowly and steadily increases its tempo. A local spirit, who descends to take possession of the trancer's body, possesses the trancer. The trance state involves a noticeable change in behavior—shivering, sometimes violent, behavior, and the name of the possessing spirit are revealed. Following the trance session are the presentations of sets of *Lakons*, or plays, by the *menora* dancers.

My wife had attended one of these dances in Penang, taken by her mother, held by Peranakan in a local town. She went every year. Mostly there were Chinese, except for a Malay man who had married a Chinese. They would attend all three days. The musical instruments would begin around 10:00 in the morning, breaking only for lunch and dinner, and quitting late, after 12:00 PM.

Everyday the "*Gaku*" in charge would go into trance, in the morning, and again in the evening, everyday of the performance. He would sit on the floor cross-legged, to enter the trance. This is a typical Malay way. He would wear a Malay shawl, chew sireh, and put Malay tobacco into his mouth. People would consult him for their problems. Donations were given voluntarily outside in a box.

Different deities would possess him—speaking Thai or Malay for the respective deities. An older brother always acted as the interpreter. The last spirit to enter him would be a tiger—crawling around the floor, picking up food that is given as offerings, and pointing at people to give the food to—so that everyone who is related to him gets something.

Tan Chee Beng also notes the presence of a "Chinese bomoh"—a spirit-doctor and magical practitioners who learned their art from the traditional Malay or Thai religious specialists. Tan expresses the conviction that "Perhaps the component of Peranakan Chinese culture that best expresses the Chineseness of the Peranakan is their Chinese religion." (1982, pg. 42)

Tan maintains that Chinese religion draws an ethnic boundary between the Peranakan Chinese and the Malays. Between the Chinese and the local Thai's, there is no such boundary between religions—"thus religion does not act as a barrier of interaction between the Chinese and the Thai." (1982. pg. 49)

It is interesting in this regard that Tan Giok-Lan's study of the Peranakan Chinese of Sukabumi, in Java, supports the thesis for the basically Chinese religious orientation of the Peranakan in general. There, patrilineal descent and patrilocality are still predominant, if flexible to local circumstances. Nowhere among the Peranakan are there deep lineage trees.

How much Chinese culture or religion presents a barrier to crossing ethnic lines, or Malay, or Chinese, or both, seems to be a matter of some conjecture—as well as what constitutes a genuinely syncretistic orientation, versus a "non-exclusive" openness to incorporate diverse elements while preserving a traditional base in belief and ritual.

The study of trance and spirit possession within the Malaysian social context reveals the differential expression of states based upon a kind of "cognitive pluralism". Stereotypes help to maintain role expectations in the performance and reactions of actors within an interethnic context.

Stereotypes and categories facilitate the process of communication of intention and significance. Cognitive diversity reflects ethnic diversity. "Social actors can respond appropriately and predictably to each other without sharing the same meanings and interpretation of events.

Complementary, reciprocal expectations of behavior—what Wallace has termed "equivalence structures"—emerge over time despite cognitive heterogeneity."(Susan K. Ackerman and Raymond Lee, "Communication and Cognitive Pluralism in a Spirit Possession Event in Malaysia", 1981:790)

Peranakan

The organization of cognitive diversity into stable role behaviors becomes problematic, and there is no necessary correspondence between collective representations and equivalence structures. Participants with a diverse range of motives and orientations share equivalence structures, and a potentially unlimited number of such equivalence structures can be 'mapped' onto collective representations.

At one level of communication, the anticipation of role behavior implies that individuals create for themselves a model of common group structure that is based upon a conception of a "generalized other." Participants can locate each other's position on a behavioral map.

Although the behavioral gestures are mutually predictable, they do not require the participants to hold the same motivations, intentions or definitions of the behaviors performed. Upon another level, people internalize these enactments and evaluate them variously and differentially, giving rise to the cognitive diversity.

Conversation between actors further modifies retrospective and on-going responses and role behaviors.

> "The sequences of complementary interaction performed on the primary level are continuously reconstructed through ongoing conversation between the participants. This reconstruction of accounts is the major mechanism by which primary-level interactions are objectified or made "real," and it extends secondary-level communication indefinitely through time. Such events as spirit possession, and their social significance, emerge as ongoing possibilities of social action from this process of communication of 'retrospective interpretations.'"
> (Ackerman and Lee, 1981: pg. 791)

Spirit possession in Malaysia has been interpreted as a traditional and culturally elaborated style of stress-management. Such spirit-possession, a popular form of entertainment in Northern Malaysia, is viewed as a symbolic representation of personality and polity that connects illness and possession to other power-laden contexts.

The symbolic language of spirit possession can be regarded as a conceptual system through which abstract power relationships (related to Malay royalty) are represented. (Kessler, 1977: 295-332)

There are a number of reactions that belong to a 'broad category" of spirit-possession in Malaysia that are not as contextually well defined or formalized as the "*main puteri*" séance.

Latah, running amok, "Malay hysteria" and mass hysteria are common instances of relatively spontaneous and uncontrolled possession which emerges suddenly in response to some discrete stimulus and involves the enactment of normally intolerable aggressive behavior "that can range from uncontrolled verbal abuse to physical violence." (Susan K. Ackerman and Raymond Lee, 1981: pg. 792)

Ethnic stereotypes emerge as inter-group "equivalence structures" in complex events of multi-ethnic spirit possession, which enable a degree of management and mutual adjustment to such events. They can be seen to function as "self-fulfilling prophecies" that mutually reinforce, and implicitly legitimize, such events. They do not direct decision-making, except perhaps indirectly, nor are they "instrumental in shaping the rules of the implicit contract."

Whatever direction social process would take, alternative equivalence structures would emerge that allow for the

mutual behavioral accommodation of the different groups—
different sets of equivalence structures would emerge from
social interaction process.

We are left to consider the role of symbols, and their
linguistic expression, in the articulation and mediation of
experience upon several parallel levels of social reality.

It is an internal dialectic of consciousness, meaning and
affect, an internal-external dialectic between internalized
frames and externally derived experience, and the dialectic
between self and other in the construction and maintenance
of psychosocial identity.

Religious symbols largely mediate the boundaries between
these different levels of experience, and provide an adaptive
mechanism for the resolution of conflict and contradiction, in
social relations, in phenomenologically derived experience, in
one's own internalized frames of reference/inference.

In this regard, ethnic symbols, and the ascriptive labels that
articulate these symbols, can be appropriated
psychologically and culturally for service of maintenance of a
sense of ego reality.

Face-to-face discourse, and the discourse functions of code
switching/mixing, serve to maintain and reinforced
internalized/external frames, to bolster ones subjective
orientation in the world, bringing this into alignment with the
objective social world.

Such symbol systems serve the function of the transmission
and mediation of cultural forms, values and orientations. In
the social construction of reality, we can speak of primary
and secondary socializations, and of possible discrepancies
between these two levels of basic and derived experience—
disjunction creates dissonance and potential conflict.

We can see in this regard ethnicity and culture working simultaneously, culture in terms of primary identity, and ethnicity in the form of secondary and derivative forms of socialization which nevertheless become internalized and have a shaping influence upon one's primary identity.

It can also be seen that several alternate, even contradictory secondary forms can become partially internalized without the concomitant level of commitment or affective, subjective identification that accompanies the subjective inevitability of primary socialization—allowing an individual to manipulate and alternate between different status-role identities and social realities.

Also, it is important to understand that the socialization process itself is always open-ended, partial and never complete—only complementary cultural closure can provide a measure of completeness and unequivocal finality to one's subjective sense of the world.

It is this fundamental unfinished quality and partiality of socialization and identification that makes secondary processes influential upon the development of personality, allowing for the possibility of both adaptive change and regressive pathology.

Finally, it is the very fact of its psychological internalization that confers such power and strength to the process. It has great realizing potency that it tends to be realized in the process of becoming internalized. Identification is likely to accompany closely internalization, and internalization is likely to accompany identification.

The social construction of reality, via symbol systems that are normatively religious, ethnically referential, and linguistically encoded, becomes the psychological reconstruction of reality that is experiential, affective, perceptual, cognitive and normative in expression, and vice versa.

IX: Baba Malay Language

One of the most visible aspects of any society is the language. "Even more striking than Malay physical appearance is the Baba's general Malay behavior: hence they not only look like Malays, but they walk, gesticulate, shake hands, eat, chew betel, sit, squat, expectorate, defecate, laugh and talk like Malays." (L. A. P. Gosling, 1964: pg. 212)

Malay, particularly the bazar or "*pasar*" ("Bazaar" Malay, has been the primary lingua franca, or "business language" of the Malay Peninsula and Indonesia between the many different ethnic groups.

Before the coming of the British, Dutch and Japanese, each of whom promoted their own language curriculum, Malay was the preferred language of choice in doing business with other people outside of one's own community.

It is therefore reasonable to expect that this dialect of "Baba Hokkien-Malay" was a primary index of acculturation and assimilation, and would have been spoken by any community that achieved some degree of successful adaptation and accommodation within the larger Malay social world.

Tan Che-Beng, in his study of the "rural Chinese" of Kelantan, notes that a partial explanation for this assimilation was the relative proximity and convenience of Malay schools and the immediate lack of availability of Chinese or English-medium schools. (Tan, 1980)

But linguistic acculturation is also a normal and expected aspect of accommodation to a host society—children acquire the socially predominant language quite naturally through indirect means, whether it is spoken in the home as a primary language or not.

The early article by Chia Cheng Sit ("The Language of the Babas" in "The Straits Chinese Magazine" Vol. II, 1898) notes that though in religion, manners, customs and though the Babas remain Chinese, for the most part they speak Baba Malay with little Chinese infusion, except for the Penang Babas. The article claims that the Baba speaks a "patois" of Malay adulterated with many borrowed idioms and words.

The grammar is greatly reduced, dropping the many particles of proper Malay speech, and, similar to Chinese, without prefixation or affixation and with the syntactical significance of words defined by their relative positioning. In somewhat condescending manner, Chia notes that the patois was sufficient for everyday business and practical matters, though insufficient for the expression of ideas on social, ethical and philosophical subjects.

A more informed linguistic analysis by Sonny Lim (1982 Baba Malay: The Language of the Straits Born Chinese Master's Thesis, Australia: Monash University), comparing Baba Malay to Pasar Malay Chitty and Portuguese Malay, places it along a continuum bridging the gap between Pasar Malay and Standard Malay. Baba Malay is primarily used intra-communally—i.e., spoken between them-selves. It is defined situationally by a number of elements, including accommodation, and is variably mixed with English and Chinese.

Literacy and illiteracy has been an important factor in the history of the language. "The Rising Star" was an awkward Baba attempt at standard Malay. The rise of Baba Malay as a lingua franca in the Eighteenth and Nineteenth Centuries reflected the economic importance of the Chinese. It represented the growth of pidginized Malay to Creole Malay featuring a syntactic reduction and simplification. Thus Baba Malay is a special creolized form of the wider form of Bazaar Malay, arising from the latter as an early pidgin or pidginized variety.

According to Lim's analysis, Baba Malay has a reduced topic-comment structure featuring the "*Punya*" article meaning literally to "possess" and is semantically related to the Hokkien form "*e*". This particle has three functions, as a possessive marker, as a marker of temporal and locative modifiers and as a relativizer, all of which correspond exactly to the Hokkien word "*e*" but which are foreign to standard Malay.

Similarly the particle "*kasi*" or "to give" is related to the Hokkien "ho" and has the same functions of benefactive, causative-benefactive, causative and passive marker. Also "*kena*" corresponds almost exactly to the Hokkien "*tio*?" with overlapping semantic fields. Similar particles include "*Mau*" (intention), "*Pigi*" (to go), "*Nanti*" (to wait) and the sentence final "la" which is originally a Hokkien form and which is an emphatic marker signaling "rapport, solidarity, familiarity and solidarity between speakers."

The word order of Baba Malay is Hokkien, in which noun phrases preceded by a marker will embed a sentence with an obligatory "*punya*" relativizer. Lim summarizes the admixture of Malay and Hokkien as strictly syntactic-semantic in nature—meanings and syntactic functions have been borrowed from Hokkien but not the forms, and mostly constitute direct substitutes for parallel and convergent Malay forms.

Lexicon is mostly Malay with Hokkien elements borrowed, which cover those Chinese aspects of Baba culture—kinship, marriage, religion, birth, death and some moral precepts. Hokkien has also modified the pronomial system.

"Baba Malay is essentially the Malay language pared down to the minimum, with the expected morphological and some syntactical features of Malay altered or missing, and with radically modified phonology" (Lim, 1982:p. 11)

The sentence structure of Baba Malay reflects the passification or topicalization, or a "topic-comment" structure of Standard Malay—in which information "is arranged such that the part of the information that is given, or the part that is already familiar, is placed at the front of the sentence (and thereby highlighting it as well)" (Ibid, p. 116)

Robert Winzeler, in his study of the village-Chinese in Kelantan, notes that these communities never completely lost use of their Chinese dialects as the Baba and Peranakan communities of the Straits and Java had, but usually became bilingual or even trilingual.

Code-switching and code-mixing is a common pattern in radically plural societies. In Penang, fused and independent bilinguals with competence in three or more languages are not unusual, but, on the contrary, are to be expected.

Ann Pakir's linguistic study of the natural discourse patterns of members of a Baba community in Singapore reveals a pattern of code-switching between Malay, Hokkien and English in which speakers attempt to negotiate "a collective social identity" and accommodate to other speaker/hearers.

I have observed extensively a similar pattern among Penang Chinese—many speakers being quite expert in code-switching/mixing between several different languages. Such linguistic skills seem to be acquired quite early and remain permanent part of speakers' linguistic facility.

Several brief studies on "Baba Malay" are extant. There seems to be about as much linguistic variation across Peranakan societies as anything else, and in general a "Peranakan" dialect can be said to rest along a continuum of creolization between mainly Hokkien, Malay or Indonesian, as well as a third or more languages, whether English, Dutch or another Chinese dialect or another regional language—for instance Siamese, or Dayak.

It appears that the degree to which Chinese or Malay is the predominant language of discourse is a measure of the extent of acculturation of the particular Peranakan community.

But for the majority of Hokkien Peranakan of Java and Malacca and Singapore, Malay appears to be the base language—"Baba Malay" is structurally and lexically the same as other vernacular dialects of Malay, with only a few phonological dialectical variations in the form of glottal stops, dipthongs, final alveolars and fricatives.

There are numerous Hokkien loan words, associated with Chinese-derived institutions, which has had otherwise relatively little effect on the phonological system (Anne Pakir, 1986) According to Pakir, Baba Malay stands as a unique dialect of Malay, in which the influence of Hokkien has been overestimated by other scholars.

Hokkien borrowings are present in extent limited to certain semantic and cultural fields, including value judgments and emotive terms. Though other Malay dialects have incorporated Hokkien terms, the way that Baba Malay uses Hokkien is unique.

According to Tan Chee-Beng, Penang Hokkien is also unique due to its Baba cultural influence, by its incorporation of many Malay words. Baba Malay spoken in Penang is also held to be different from the variety spoken in Malacca and elsewhere because of the greater influence of Hokkien and English.

The Hokkien of Kelantan that is spoken by the "village Chinese" is also dialectically distinct in intonational patterns, due to the alleged influence of Malay and Siamese.

Victor Purcell, in his book The Chinese in Malaya (1948), declares that Baba Malay is different from Malay in many important respects, and is "practically a different language". He states that a great many Malay words are unknown to the Babas, as well as the "more polished syntax of the Malay. They are ignorant of the words connected with the Mohammedan religion. Also they mispronounce many Malay words..." (Purcell, 1948, pg. 294)

He goes on to state that the greatest divergence between Baba Malay and Malay is in its construction, in which the former follows the Chinese pattern in a reduced form. It is possible that the sources of data between Ann Pakir's analysis and that of Victor Purcell, or Rev. Shellabear's, are different, reflecting substantial areal variations and dialectical differentiation in the pattern of the 'patois' as different speakers range along different parts of the continuum.

If Purcell's interpretation was accurate, it would reflect speakers who are using Chinese as the basolect, and Malay as the mesolect. On the other hand, Pakir's source suggests just the reverse—Malay remains the base language only slightly modified by the superimposition of Hokkien lexicon.

It is evident that Purcell based part of his study on the earlier study made by Reverend W. G. Shellabear, published in the Journal of the Straits Branch of the Royal Asiatic Society, (Vol. 65, 1913), which was reprinted as an appendix in John Clammer's work Straits Chinese Society (1980). Shellabear emphasizes the influence of the Chinese idiom, and the distinctiveness of Baba Malay from either the High Malay of the literature of the Malay Peninsula, or the low Malay spoken in Indonesia.

"It is true that the number of Chinese words which have become assimilated with this dialect is not very large, and that many words have been borrowed from English, Portuguese, Dutch and Tamil, and from other neighboring tongues, but it is rightly called 'Baba Malay,' for it is largely the creation of the Baba Chinese, and is their mother tongue, so that it belongs to them in a sense that no other people can or do claim it as their own." (Tan Chee Beng, 1980: pg. 156)

Tan Chee-Beng; takes a more restrictive definition of Baba Malay as that dialectic spoken by the Baba's of Malacca, that became the "business dialect" of the three Straits Settlements—Penang, Malacca and Singapore.

The Malay learned by members of each of these settlements was dialectically different—and the bazaar Malay, or "*Melayu pasar*" from which Baba Malay developed was a lingua franca for commerce.

Hokkien loan words are more salient in areas of customs, religion and kinship, for things related to the house, furniture, food, utensils, personal effects and other things. "In general it may be said that Chinese loanwords are used mostly for things and concepts which are of Chinese origin or which have no Malay equivalents." (Tan Chee-Beng, 1980: 156)

Maurice Freedman, who made an important study of the kin terms in Baba Malay, states that: "in general, Malay words were used for junior relative and Hokkien-derived terms for senior. And this usage appears to correspond with that of the analogues of the Babas across the water in Java, the

Peranakan

Peranakan, among whom both Malay and Javanese terms come into play for junior relatives." (Freedman, "Chinese Kinship and Marriage in Singapore," 1962)

Tan Chee Beng concludes by noting that "Linguistic acculturation does not necessarily mean that a people have to speak the same dialect or language of the "host" group. In fact, a new dialect may develop, giving the people a distinct dialect which also serves as a crucial symbol of ethnic identity..."(1980:165)

Language serves as one of the most important agents and vehicles social integration. In a plural context, it can be both a barrier and a facilitator to interethnic interactions. Racial, ethnic, and class differences are all reflected in linguistic differences, and linguistic difference is an important indicator of an individual's social status, orientation toward the larger social world, background, and ability to successfully interact in the world.

The contribution of a unique genre of Peranakan literature from Java is noteworthy—it is a genre of fictional novels, poems and plays that has not been well studied. The Baba's of Singapore made their own contribution to Peranakan literary development in the form of stories translated from the Chinese and English in Baba Malay, newspaper and journal articles, as well as a few original works in English. "Baba Malay literature continued to be printed in Singapore until about the Second World War." (Maurice Freedman, 1962)

John Clammer points to several interrelated social factors in the relative paucity of this literature. Many Peranakan up until the turn of the century were basically illiterate. Furthermore, as an interstitial community, there was a fundamental ambivalence of cultural identity that precluded any such great literary florescence—even what language to primarily publish in Chinese, Baba Malay or English, remained a critical "trilemma."

Due to the basic ambiguity of their cultural identity "at the nexus of three civilizations" and their lack of any clear political culture, except that framed by the colonial administration, the Peranakan lacked the appropriate developmental or cultural context conducive to the cultivation of a refined literature.

"The mutual reinforcement of socio-political-cultural and literary values of this kind was absent from Straits Chinese society at its outset. Indeed, what Peranakan culture had to do was to find or create precisely such a nexus of interrelated influences..." (John Clammer, 1980: 68)

X: The Story of Precious Moon

The following true account is by a descendant of the Nonya tradition in Penang, given as a clear example of a "mosaic" ethno-culture. The names have been changed to protect the identity of those still living and the memory of those since passed. It is important in the understanding of this tradition to learn how its distinctive sense of ethno-culture had become articulated in the subjective experiences of the individual culture bearer. It is important to understand how such experience may actually have been shaped by culture, and how we in turn might shape that sense of tradition and impart it upon our descendants.

Peranakan society, wherever it had taken root and flourished, wherever it had spread its seed, always had its own sense of order, organization, purpose and outlook upon the world. It has long had its hopes for the future espoused in its own way of bringing up its youngest generation, and a sense of present importance with the generation that has come of age in the world, and an orientation toward the past that is passing away with the oldest.

What are your earliest memories of your grandma?

She was gray, her clothes always looked dirty, her hair was always in a mess—ends always coming out from her sanggul. Thinning. I remember her long nails too. I will probably get a nightmare about her tonight. Every time I visited her I remember her lying down in a sway-backed bed, or in the kitchen. She was probably in her late seventies then, very old. Must have been born in the eighteen hundreds—1890, around there. I can only trace as far back as my grandmother. Can't help get the feeling of old. She would usually give me a dollar if I let her hold me or touch me, which I wouldn't do because she was so old and dirty. I was such a young girl—five years old. She'll call; she'll say "lai, lai, chu, chu, amah sayang" I would usually try to get away from her. They'd let her touch me once. I only wanted that dollar. Then I' d run off, scared. I really didn't know her that well as a grandmother. Maybe because she was so independent, she didn't want to stay with us. She would only stay in her "kong chu" her ancestor's house—the house that she bought, the house that she was raised in, had children in, that her son and husband lived in. Also her youngest sister lived there, in spite of the fact that the house was old, dilapidated, the atap had holes, had coconut oil lamps. She had no running water. Only had electricity for her tenets—one bulb. Had to go outside to get water. No bathroom—an outside. She was so stingy with her money; she didn't want anyone to pay for it. There was only one tiny red bulb—so dim you can't even see your hand in front of you. Pretty stingy, huh. The only thing I could get out of her was that one dollar, too.

You want me to tell you where she kept all her secret money—in cigarette cans. In those days they didn't buy packets of cigarettes—they would buy only a cigarette at a time to smoke, so the cigarettes were sold in the can—50 to a can at the sundry shop. I can remember the brands—"Rough Rider,"" Kraven A,"" Torchlight," there's a few more but I don't remember them—their name escapes me. I remember one. It had a sailor and an Anchor on the can. She'd put all her money in there—her dollar notes, her jewelry, and then she'd put them all in a cupboard. She had those gold coins—minted gold coins. She didn't believe in banks. She never put her money in banks. She'd put them in her cupboard—soot stained. She'd lock the cupboard with a key that she'd keep around her neck all the time. The string was so black with her perspiration. She's so cheap she'd use the outer layers of coconut that would create a lot of smoke. Her pots were all black. You could never get it clean, either. All those years of accumulated soot. Poor old lady. I don't know why she would never come to live with us. My mother would try to make her come to live with us. I don't think she trusted my mom, either. I don't think she trusted anybody.

Why don't you think she trusted people?

From what I understand, she only had one son, who was the apple of her eye. I think it would have been a different story if he had lived, but he died real young—left a wife and child. I think when her son died, her world died with him. I know she didn't care for her two daughters, my mom and my aunt. She had a saying. —"Daughters are ashes—you can't kindle a fire with ashes—whereas a son is kindling." A daughter is nothing—your name goes down through your son—your son is more important. She always says that to my mom and her sister.

How about her husband?

Well her husband and her never did get along. Always fighting with him over trivial things—she was always domineering, aggressive and bossy, never a very loving person—in her younger days she wasn't very loving toward her children or her husband. You want me to tell you the incident that broke my Grandfather's back. My grandfather wanted to go into business with a friend of his. But he didn't have the cash on him, because my grandmother held the purse strings, all the money was with her. So he asked money from her, but she wouldn't give it to him. She made a big fuss. So he got very angry. "You don't have to give me the money, but I'm going to my store and I'm not coming back to you. I'll send you money for you to buy food, but I'm not coming back to live as husband and wife with you. There wasn't talk of divorce or separation. Where he had his business, a few miles away. He'd send money with his friend, but he never did stay in the house. He never went into business with his friend, because my grandmother wouldn't allow it.

You know what kind of business he had?

I don't know—I think it was by the sea—so I think it had something to do with fishing: selling supplies, fishing nets, gear, that sort of thing.

My grandmother was very frugal, to the point of being stingy. My grandfather was more "chin chai"—more easy going. I think he was hen-pecked by her. My mother told me when my grandfather moved out, my grandmother would not go to visit him. Friends would come to take my mom to visit him. I remember she said how much fun she had there. She could run around. She was only about ten and my aunt about six. And then when people would come to say "its time to go home," they would always cry and cry, they wanted to stay with him.

What do you think ever happened to her money?

She hoarded it. She had money. Jewelry. I think she bought gold. After my grandfather died, she must have spent a little because she had to live on it. She had a lot of money. After she died, the story goes, the bulk, 99% of everything was to go to the grandson—the son of the son that had died. My mother received a few things, my aunt, and nieces, inherited a few pieces of jewelry. But the grandson—the house, the land, inherited the bulk, everything went to him. It was supposed to go to the grandson. But I heard strange things happened to the gold and the money. This is like family skeleton. Are you ready? According to my mom, after my grandmother had passed away, they opened her cupboard where she kept all her things, there was only a little bit of jewelry and a little bit of cash, most of her stuff was missing. She figured that since my grandmother trusted the old man Chan, he probably opened the cupboard and taken some things out. Like old man Chan had access to her body—anyone could have swiped her key and taken a few cans of her stuff. She had to have cash, she collected rent, she didn't believe in banks. Old man Chan was a pretty high gambler in those days—he probably just gambled it away. I wouldn't put it past him. I think he's got that streak in him that he would do it. Anyway the bulk of it went to her grandson. I should say my cousin, but he's so old we think of him as our uncle.

Now the grandson at that time was in Australia, going to medical school. His mother was working in KL so his mother came up to Penang and acted as a caretaker for his house while he finished his study. But the strange thing was the son never came back, he married an Australian and stayed there. The mother was left holding the property. She took over what Grandmother had then, collecting rent—-some Indians had made homes under the house—Malay style house on stilts— they made cubicles. A Chinese had rented a piece of the property to build a house on it. They were there a long time since my grandmother, paying rent. Very minimum—like 60 dollars. Then there was an Indian sundry shop on the property—30 or 40 dollars. Then another Indian built a little shack where he could put his personal things—just a corrugated pine shack. He had a small business in Pulau Tikos selling ice. Then there was another Indian couple. I think the husband pulled the cart—manpower. He was that. An odd job kind of laborer. They had built themselves a little shack there, too. Underneath the house, there was a big space that wasn't being used—Anyone that didn't have a home would stay there—any one time there were four or five men staying there. She would charge them rent too. That's where Elgin, the old man Chan, everyone picked up Tamil. So this lady sort of inherited all this.

Is this the house your Mom lived in?

Yes, when she grew up she lived there. Where I lived too until I was two years old. Then we moved from there.

Did your father live in the same house?

No, remember my father had a first wife. He couldn't come visit.

So that's what happened to the money—this women, we call her Akim, took over.

She didn't like my Mom or aunt. She liked only her son, who had an education. My mother stayed at home and worked a lot. They weren't abused, but if they didn't tow the line they'd get beatings. My mother had to collect coconuts, grate them. It was a pan— huge chunk at a time. My grandmother burned coconut oil. They had to wash, clean, everything, lah, these young ladies had to do. I think my mother and her sister were very close. They were like each other's support group. And then they'd have to shuffle the Chi Ki cards whenever her friends came over—one of those card games the old Nonyas would play. She'd have to make coffee, run out and buy like an errand girl. Everyday they'd have to stay up late until they stopped playing, they'd practically fall asleep on the gambling table. People would poke them to wake them up. They'd be paid twenty cents—that was a lot of money in those days—the 30's. Life was very hard for them. They had to do a lot, sweep the Kampong, collect the chicken eggs. I think when my aunt got married; my mom was pretty much devastated, because she wasn't there anymore. I remember when my aunt got married. My grandmother arranged it—sent out all these feelers. I don't think my aunt was aware it was going that fast. Next day, "well, you're getting married!" My aunt didn't see the groom before they got married. And she was devastated. She was crying for a few days, because she said her husband was so ugly, dark and black—on account he worked for this ship plying between Penang and Sumatra. I think he was in the Charcoal trade. My aunt was very beautiful. She was crying, and asked my Grandmother why she did it. And my grandmother says, "you've got to go to your husband, you can't come home anymore." That's about all I know of my aunt too. I called her "Ma-ee"—" Auntie Mommy". That's as much as I know about my aunt. I guess my mother was alone after that.

My mother told me that relatives came from Taiping. She went to stay with them there and she had a wonderful time. The father owned a bottling factory—she could drink all the soda she wanted. Those days there was a marble that would fall into the soda when it was opened. She'd drink it to see the marble floating there, and get sick on it. They both had pretty hard lives. They still had to work. I think the war came a couple of years after she got married.

You don't know anything else about your grandmother?

I just know she wasn't a very pleasant lady. For example, she had cataracts and my mom made her go to the hospital. My mom would come to her everyday. She would bitch—"I want to go home to see my things." My mom told her she would come stay with her after the hospital. She fixed everything up at the house. After the first day—she would complain to go home. So my mom said go on. My father took her home. I've got to go home to see Pau Kim. That's Chan's name. She trusted the old man Chan more than her own children—being the only man in the family; they kind of depended on him a lot. They trusted him, which they shouldn't have. He kind of hypnotized her. I think that's how he got her money. Old man Chan always told us that our mother cheated his mother out of their share of the house. He never worked much. I guess working for the British had something to do with it. Gave him a sense of self-importance. I think if he had been more manly about it, he would have been a con man. He would help his wife with the laundry—in the Chinese clan he would be the laughing stock of all the men—but he would do that.

He wasn't a Baba?

He is. His mother was the nicest old lady you ever met. I call her Apo. She was very soft-spoken old lady. Nicer than my grandmother. She wouldn't give us money, but she had a chicken and would give each of us a chicken egg. Give each of us a Kampong egg. Would tell my mother—"you must never beat your children"—"you must love and cherish your children." Her husband left her. He was supposed to be a Kapitan China, who came from Perak. That's what old man Chan always tells me. Apo was his first wife. His father was a womanizer; I guess he didn't love Apo. After old man Chan was born, went back to Perak, settled down with another woman, and had children. On the other hand, the husband was such a womanizer and had given Apo a venereal disease. She had some kind of skin condition on both her legs from knee down. Holes and puss and festering wounds, both feet were swollen. Everyday clean them. My Apo clean both her legs, use some leaves for medicinal purpose—role them up and poke the sores to drain them out. Every time she does that it grossed me out. Think how a nice person like that could produce a son like that. She had nice no pretensions—nice old lady.

Peranakan

Old man Chan had an adopted sister—Apo bought her after her
husband left her. She married a Malay guy. Old man Chan
pushed her around, and kicked her out because he didn't want
her to marry a Malay guy. She married him anyways. After that
she was practically cut off, she couldn't come home to see her
mother. Old man Chan forbid her to put her feet on her doorway.
I guess after many years he relented—she let her come visit her
mother. Well, that's about it.

Do you remember your grandmother's surname?

Toh, T, O, H. I think they came from Burma. She was very dark
complected. She didn't have a Chinese face—very dark
complexion. She had a Mongol face—very prominent high
cheek bones. Not oval but her face was very long. Very strong
features. I remember her ears were very long. I remember her in
a picture wearing the "paju pangong," she had a handkerchief
over her shoulder. That picture belongs to Chan's wife. I
remember seeing that picture.

You say she comes from Burma?

She might have some Burmese blood in her. Her father may
have come down from Burma. My mother mentioned it a few
times. She might have some family in Burma. Even her mother
may have been Burmese, but I never heard her speak Burmese
before. She was very dark, very masculine features. She doesn't
look feminine. She was pretty dirty. Old man Chan told me she
could go into trance, she could be possessed by "Nanat"-—
Malay spirit—a woman's spirit. She told me that one time she
went into a trance, and the spirit told her that my mother was
possessed by the devil, so she started hitting her with a stick to
drive it out. She didn't do it very often, but she could go into a
trance.

Do you think she latah'd?

No, I don't think so. But I think my Apo can—kind of borderline, say a few words, like that. I didn't know her well. She died when I was five. She wasn't close to us, except Seh Bahn who could whittle her money out from her. She wasn't like a grandmother.

So what about your Mom?

Well, she always wore the Sarong and the sleeveless tops for everyday wear, except when she goes out or to functions she wore her Kerbaya. As long as I ever saw her, she wore that. I know she liked to sing her Malay songs. She would tell us that when her brother's wife would come, she would try to teach them the alphabet, but my grandmother would put a stop to it real fast-"they're dumb, why bother?" I know that she was very close to her sister.

When my aunt got sick she took my aunt to the hospital, the doctor told her she had cancer of the uterus. My mother was so upset, because the doctor showed her what it looked like. My aunt knew about it, and she was so depressed. Well, she died. I think in 1959-60. It was a grand funeral. Everybody came. I remember it. My grandmother didn't go. I guess losing a daughter was painful to her. Before she had died, she asked my mother to keep an eye on her children. When she goes she will be happy. Every week or so the children would come and visit us. My mother was much closer to the second daughter—still young, and the little boy. The oldest daughter was already married. The second daughter was going out with a young guy that the father didn't approve of. My mother was like a go between. Every time my mother would have to go convince my uncle he was O.K. He gave his daughter a really hard time. He finally relented. Finally, my mom was insulted, because she let her father's sister do all the arranging. She didn't do any of it. She said she didn't carry through what she had promised her dead sister. She didn't go to the wedding. When a Chinese sends out invitations to a wedding, they send the parents to issue the invitations. But since her mother was dead, and her father's sister had taken over the arrangements, then her aunt

should have personally come to issue the invitation—she didn't
do it, she didn't show respect to her mother. She felt slighted
over that, since she was the next best thing to her mother. It's
like my mother was cut off at that point. It was like a slap in the
face for her, no recognition. After that she didn't have anything
to do with them for a long time. They moved to Sarawak for
three years. She visited my mom again when she returned.
They started communicating again. I think they had a very
modern wedding, with the white veil. Even Seh Bahn had a very
western one, not a traditional wedding.

What else about your Mom?

She like to play the Chi Ki. She also like the Mah Jong. She
could read the Mah Jong characters on the cards. She knew
English perfectly well, she could understand whatever you told
her, but she just couldn't speak it. She spoke very good Malay—
excellent Malay, I should say. She spoke Hokkien. She loved
the "Dondang Sayang." She loved that. Then she love Boria.
The Boria is very Penang. It's like a group of people, usually just
men, invited to social functions and they have to sing songs that
praise somebody—like a millionaire who gives charity. Sing
songs for five minutes. It can be anything—an animal, a person.
It's very Penang, traditionally only a Penang thing. Now it's all
over Malaysia. She loved Malay movies because she spoke
Malay so well. She also loved Hindi and Tamil movies. Once in
a while she'd go to traditional Hokkien songs, like the Hokkien
opera. As long as it's Hokkien she likes to watch it. A very
generous person. Always helping one person and the next.
Always helping someone—feed them and clothe them. In fact,
old man Chan's sister, who married a Malay guy, my mom
supported them for ten years. The whole family stayed with us.
The husband, wife, two children. They didn't give my mom a
single cent. Her husband was a gambler. Owed money right and
left. They were so destitute they couldn't afford food. My mother
had a thing, wouldn't tell them when to leave. My father would
say, well whose new here today. She was a real homemaker.

She'd have four children of the first wife to live with us at a time. I think the last four. There were always four or five children from my husband's first wife staying with us. Then people would always conveniently drop by for lunch and dinner. Everyday she'd go to the market and buy food. She'd have a huge basket and buy ten dollars worth of food. It could feed twenty people at the time. She'd buy a big gantang of rice—a gunney sack. Everyday she'd cook, lunch and dinner. She'd have old man Chan, sister's mother-in-law, grandchildren, sister's husband and children. Always a houseful of people. She always did this. She didn't resent these people coming in again and sponging off her. If you can find a more delicate term for it. Of course she would have, like on weekends, on Saturday and Sunday, my father would come home from the Turf Club, horse racing, he would take us out to dinner—my mom's day off was Saturday and Sunday. Usually I got to go. He'd take us to this restaurant called Lok Tai Ki. He always ordered the same thing—bowl of soup, curry, and fried salted fish for me, and then there would always be a bowl of sambal balachan.

What else can I say about my Mom? She was a good cook. A fantastic cook. Everyday cooked Nonya food. Everyday must have curry, sambal. She had a pounder this big. She always had one hot dish everyday. She liked to have animals—always buying baby chicks and ducklings. She loved her chickens and ducks. We never bought eggs. She kept two geese, two turkeys too. She just kept them.

She arranged my sister's wedding. She found the groom for her. Got them together. They went out a few times, and presto, they're getting married. It was arranged. That's why Seh Bahn is so bitter. The husband came and lived with her. It was a "Chin Choi"—literally to "marry into the bride's family"—you don't have to pay for anything, everything is taken care of. They lived with her for five or six years until my parents broke up.

She spoke very good Malay. But when she spoke Hokkien she would put Malay words into it. She'd say "Tolong" a lot—"help"—

Peranakan

"Tolong mama Sai Chi"— "Help mommy with the vegetables." I cannot give you examples, examples is hard to give.

She's into the deity scene. Always going around to the deities. The Dato, the Keramat, she'd be there. She wouldn't trance. She liked to go around the temples.

She ate the betel leaves—the sireh—the sireh leaves with the gambier. But she didn't chew tobacco. Thank god for that. But she smoked! Her packet of cigarettes—10 to a packet—would last her two, two and a half days.

She had a lot of friends, but nobody did anything for her when she died. Come this year it will be 10 years since she died.

Would she keep her money like your Grandma?

She'd keep her money. Not in a can, but between her clothes. She didn't keep it in the bank. She didn't trust them. I don't think she'd know how to negotiate with the banker. Seh Bahn kept her money at home up until the time when my niece started working, now they have a joint bank account. She wouldn't do it with the son; she wouldn't trust him. They would love their sons, but they wouldn't trust them. Betty (my niece) is always very frugal. She saves her money and when she wants something she buys it.

She likes to play the Tong Tin, like the Vietnamese play. A rotating credit circle. We call it Tong Tin. Sometimes it would go for three years—two years, a year and a half. The short ones would go for a year. Sometimes twenty people. Usually 20 dollars a month. That would be my mother's share. So you figure if she had three Tong Tins going at one time she needs to save seventy dollars a month to pay. Sometimes she'd have two or three going at one time, so she had to really keep track of them so she'd have the money when the leader comes and collects it from her. She liked to play the number game with the magical number book. She was totally illiterate, she couldn't read or write.

So tell me about your sister?

What do you want to know about her? She got married real young, maybe seventeen years old. She didn't have a choice. It was a match thing, you know. But at least she met her husband before they were officially engaged. I remember my father threw her an engagement party. My grandmother was still alive though when she got engaged. She died the same year, so the Chinese have a tradition, you have to get married within a hundred days of the death, if not you have to wait three years. So within three months my sister got married. It was a big wedding. We didn't go to those big fancy restaurants. My mother had a "chong por"—come in and cook for all the guests. He did the cutting up, in charge of the kitchen. And then also my mother had a "*ch'ng kek em*"—he's the one that knows the prayers, how to make up the bride. She's the one that also provides the wedding dress. It was a white one. A very western wedding. My sister also wore white. Like three days before the wedding the "ch'ng kek em" came from Kulin and she brought with her the wedding dress, and then she would have to "kui bin" ceremony on my sister. It's where they shave off all the hair of the face by using boiled egg yolk, then they cut the fringe, and then they put on cosmetic for the first time, like the rouge, eyebrow, first time. All the brides have to go through that. I remember I was curious and wanted to see it. But every one said "shh, shhh, you're a little girl, you can't see". But they never explained why. "Little children cannot see but you'll know when you get married." Because he was a "Chin Choi," the bridegroom didn't have to give anything. The bride's parents paid for the wedding. I guess my parents gave the bride some gold jewelry, but that's about it. He was originally from Singapore. And then, I remember they had a night before the wedding, a lot of people came over. My father threw an informal dinner for relatives and close friends. And then my sister, at a special time they had someone look up the time, and she prayed to the god's. The "ch'ng kek em" helped her with all that. My parents fed Seh Bahn the sweet rice balls cooked in syrup. They fed her that, I remember that. I do not remember much of the wedding itself. Only people coming and going. My sister looked so beautiful in her bridal dress. My parents before asked her to put on her wedding wreath—they put it on for her and the "Ch'ng kek em" will do the rest. That's all I remember.

Does your sister ever wear the kebaya?

I've never seen her wear the kebaya. She's always in a western dress. And then her husband moved in with her. And then Betty came along nine month's later. They had the baby, and my mother hired an "*orang jaga*" to take care of the baby and to cook for the mother, wash for the mother and take care of her. That one-month period is special confinement for the mother so she has to have special food cooked and all that.

I remember Betty as an infant. As a neonate when they brought her back from the hospital. I remember the "orang jaga" was there. I remember I was so interested in what they were doing to the baby—bath her, change her, powder her bottom, and then they'd wrap her up so tightly she could not move. And the baby would sleep with the "orang jaga." My sister didn't have to take care of the baby because the "orang jaga" was there. She didn't have to cook or get up in the middle of the night for the baby. She was lucky in a since, not like me.

Does your sister cook Nonya food?

Yes, yes, they eat a lot of sambal balachan; curries, gulai. She likes hot food. Even Betty likes that, but she likes soup too. Betty doesn't care for hot food that much. My sister only went to school until grade six. Seems she played hooky a lot. She was good, but she just wasn't interested in being in school. My mother sent her to the convent school at Pulau Tikos—a Christian school. She even went to church a few times but my grandmother was shocked. I get the feeling she was influenced by the Convent school, because they had to say mass every morning and say prayers before they go to class, so she followed that. She dropped out after grade six. She'd make Lau

Mak carry her piggy back to school. When she would act up she'd make her carry her piggyback style. My sister was naughty when she was young because grandmother spoiled her. She was my grandmother's favorite. She could get away with a lot with my grandmother. I don't know when this happened, but she was a young girl. She got on this man's bicycle that was high in the compound. Olive put her on the bicycle and let go and she rode right through one of the tenant's shacks—right through the front door. She hit her head on the corrugated metal roof and cut her head on it. She bled a lot and until this day you can see the cut. My grandmother got really upset with Olive for that. Another time she was a ring leader, some of the tenant's children, and Tony, they went to the Toddy shop and bought themselves a pint of Toddy, took it home and went under the house and started drinking the Toddy and got drunk on the Toddy without anyone knowing about it. She loved curry when she was a little girl and she didn't want to eat what my Mom or Lau Mak cooked and she'd go around to the tenants and they'd feed her rice and curry. She speaks Malay, but not very good. Not as fluent as my mother.

Now she is just a housewife. She saves her money. She's rich I tell you. She's like my grandmother, very frugal. She can make a dollar out of fifty cents. Whatever she can she saves. She buys gold. She even has a safety deposit box chock full of her gold things. Now she's just a housewife, not a very happy housewife. She knows "Chi Ki", but never plays it. I've seen her play a few times with her mother, when she was younger. She goes to the Kramats. In fact she still goes to the one my mother used to go to. The manora. My mom would go three times a year. She goes to the same places.

What about yourself?

You know. I was the youngest in the family. I guess I was spoiled. I was still punished severely when I was naughty. I guess Americans would say I was abused. I still got caning and the pinching. I remember the worst one in my life. My mother locked me outside and let me cry and cry. I was only five or six years old. Maybe five. In the morning until my father came home from lunch. That must have been traumatic because I remember it still. I would get to go everywhere with my parents. I was the only one they would take. On the weekends when my father came home from the Turf club, he would take us to dinner. I remember lots of toys from the Turf club. I remember he bought me a nice toy pram, and then one time he bought me a magician's box, and then one time he bought me a buy and sell box with little scales for weighing up things. Those were the nice few things he bought me. I remember that. Then if he came home drunk, he'll let me go through all the pockets and take all the loose change. Sometimes there would be three or four dollars of loose change. I was rich. Sometimes I would watch those little scenes on TV if a man got drunk they'd put hot compresses on the head. I'd do that a lot, acted nurse for my dad. We'd go on weekends. Just travel. To Butterworth, Ipoh, Taiping. Spend the day with relatives and then come back the same day. He was pretty relaxed with the kids but my mom was the strict disciplinarian. She was good when she was good, but when she was bad she was bad. I pretty much had a very normal childhood—nothing much until the teens. Teenagers always have problems anyway—insecure, you always don't feel good about yourself, and all that.

How about Betty?

Well when Betty was growing up I thought she was a pest. Maybe I was a little jealous. I had center stage so long, and then she came along and took the stage. There's only six years between us, not a lot. When she was growing up, my mom was the one who took care of her. Seh Bahn didn't do a lot of that, after the "Ch'ng kek em" left. Betty would sleep with all of us. Follow my mom and dad everywhere. Seh Bahn was the mother but that was it. My mom would let her play with my toys and books and she would tear them all up. I got real mad at that. As she grew old, I guess we got closer and closer, she began to catch up with me. Pretty soon we were real close. She's like my little sister. A very nice girl.

When the Malay boy friend was going out with her, her parents gave her a hard time. They didn't like that. Her father gave her a hard time. Nothing came of it anyway. At least I don't think so. Peter is pretty much the spoiled one. He gets away with a lot. He gripes and in the end they always give in to him. I think they love Peter a little more. His mother brought him up. My mother didn't take care of her. He was much closer to them than Betty was.

Seh Bahn has never done a lot. Always close to home. She's lucky. Everything is taken care of for her. Until she got into her thirties, then she had to do a lot for herself. But before then she was very dependent on my mother and father. Very stingy, lah. Too stingy for words. I don't think I'm that way. That's why I don't save money. I have my gold, but that's about it. She doesn't have any friends. The only friends she has belong to my mother's age group. Her own age group, she doesn't have any. She knows the rules to cards, but she doesn't play them. She's cut-off from the world. She's lonely. If it weren't for Betty. I think she lives for Betty; she's so attached to her, hanging on to her. My sister is sad—she's not happy with her life. Her marriage isn't good. I don't think her husband really loves her. There's no love between them. She doesn't have any friends. The only person she can relate to besides her daughter is me, and I'm eight thousand miles away.

Do you miss Betty?

Yes. I think it would be nice to have her around. But, no can do.

I get the impression that the Nonyas are very domestic and it persists from Mother to daughter?

I think the women are the only ones who maintain the bond of being "Nonya." If a group of Nonya's came here they would still

Peranakan

be the same way—"What is the women's movement" or "Women's lib," I still take care of my own family. They are very much family oriented. Family is very important to them. Their children; their husband. In that order too, I think. When the children come along, the husband sort of takes a second place. The men have always kind of protected them, so the woman is always at home. The daughter's are raised to be the same way. It's passed on from mother to daughter. The sons go out and go to school. The women are the one's who carry the whole thing. Not the men. I never hear anything about the men.

They don't wear Malay clothes; they wear Chinese clothes. Basically the only Malay thing that the men ever do is eat sambal balachan. Look at my sister, she is the same way. But Betty is not that way because she has to go out and work.

The world is changing now—you just can't do it any more that way. Even for myself—I had to go out to work, in the 70s. It stopped at my sister, who grew up in the fifties and got married in 1963. There's no more Nonya culture—which is a sad thing. It kind of died out. The women don't sit around in their groups and play Chi Ki, chew sireh leaves, talk about food and their families. That's all gone. It's sad in a way, and in another way it's just the change of the times. You cannot live in the past; women do not do that anymore.

You're pretty much a "home-body" too?

Yes I am. I'm proud to be a homebody, so hoots to anybody who says otherwise. For me, my family comes first. It is very important to me. I'm sorry if a lot of people disagree with that. It's the opposite of people who think it's very "unliberated"—not what a "modern woman" should be. Every one is entitled to their opinion. It's just that my choice is to be at home with my family. My career is my family—that's a career. Personally I think it's a very important career. My mother was a homebody, my sister is a homebody, my Grandmother was a homebody, and they didn't turn out bad. They may have had problems, but who doesn't.

Since this is representing you, is there anything else you want to say about the Nonyas?

I think it's a shame that it's dying. There's no such thing as pure Nonya culture and customs anymore. I would like to have my daughter learn about it. What I know is so minimum, it won't help her to learn a lot, except teaching her how to cook. I retain that part. The customs, culture, are all gone. Some of my thoughts are still very Nonya. My outlook on life is also that way too. I resent the fact that some Chinese, when they ask me—Do you know Mandarin?" or "Do you know which part of China your Ancestor's come from?"—I reply: "No, I don't, I only know Malay and English and my own Hokkien dialect." I get the feeling that though they make a polite reply, they deep down feel like "What an odd ball, she doesn't even know Mandarin." I resent the Malays, how they are treating the Chinese population there. The policies are not fair. The Chinese are being pretty much discriminated against, economically as well as politically. I think with the policies being that way, I feel very Chinese when the discrimination is against my own people. Then I don't feel very Nonya any more.

A Comprehensive, Annotated Bibliography on Peranakan Studies

A.

Ackerman, S. E. & Raymond M. Lee
    1981 "Communication and Cognitive Pluralism in
        a Spirit Possession Event in Malaysia"
        <u>American Ethnologist.</u>

Outlines spirit possession events in northern
Malaysia, specifically instances of mass hysteria
involving Malay factory women, comparing these to
ritually ordered trance, and discusses how these
events are managed, manipulated, and mediated
through ethnic stereotypes and interethnic
expectations in ongoing communication.

    1988 <u>Heaven in Transition: Non-Muslim Religious</u>
        <u>Identity and Ethnic Identity in Malaysia</u>
        Honolulu: Univ. of Hawaii Press

A brief descriptive study dealing with contemporary
religious movements in modern Malaysia, and the
relation of ethnicity in participants' involvement with
these social phenomena.

B.

Balibain, John

1932 <u>Hail, Penang!</u> ?
An old work by a British colonial administrator. It contains an interesting description of Chinese courtship and marriage customs, and is interesting from the standpoint of the colonial history of Penang.

Bastin, John; & R Roolvink, editors.
1964 <u>Malayan and Indonesian Studies: Essays Presented to Sir Richard Winstedt on his Eighty-Fifth Birthday</u> Oxford: Clarendon Press.

Blumberg, Paul, editor.
1972 <u>The Impact of Social Class</u> New York: Thomas Y. Crowell Co.

Bonacich, Edna
1980 "Middleman Minorities and Advanced Capitalism" <u>Ethnic Groups</u>, Vol. 2: 211-219.

Braddel, T
1850a "Notices of Penang" <u>Journal of the Indian Archipelago.</u>

1851b "Notices of Penang" <u>Journal of the Indian Archipelago.</u>

1852c "Notices of Penang" <u>Journal of the Indian Archipelago.</u>

1857d "Notices of Penang" <u>Journal of the Indian Archipelago.</u>

Peranakan

1855e "Notes on the Chinese of the Straits"
Journal of the Indian Archipelago.

1856f "Notes on Malacca"
Journal of the Indian Archipelago, n.s. 1

Bromley, Yu V.
1978 On the Typology of Ethnic Communities

Brown, D. E.
1976a Principles of Social Structure: Southeast
Asia Westview Press, Inc.

An insightful and well written social anthropological
study of a theory of corporate social organization
based upon alternative "principles" such as
ethnicity, kinship, occupation, etc., using case
studies drawn from Southeast Asia.

1964b Southeast Asia: Its Historical Development
New York, N.Y.: McGraw Hill Book Co.

C.

Clammer, John
1979a The Ambiguity of Identity: Ethnicity
Maintenance and Change Among the
Straits Chinese Community of Malaysia and
Singapore Institute of Southeast Asian
Studies Occasional Paper, #54 Singapore:
University of Singapore Press.

1980b Straits Chinese Society Singapore:
Singapore Univ. Press

A key reference text treating the sociology of the Straits Chinese, based in part upon statistical studies done in Malacca, contesting some of the common "folk-stories" of Matrilocality and intermarriage among the Babas and Malays. Contains an excellent, exhaustive bibliographic review of literature relating to the Peranakan, a study of Peranakan Literature, as well as a reprint of the 1914 article by Rev. Shellabear on the Baba Malay dialect.

1983 "Studies in Chinese Folk Religion in Singapore and Malaysia" Contributions to Southeast Asian Ethnography, John Clammer, Editor, No. 2, August. Singapore: National University of Singapore.

Coedes, George
    1968 The Indianized States of Southeast Asia Honolulu, Hawaii: East-West Center Press

Coppel, Charles A.
    1983 Indonesian Chinese in Crisis Kuala Lumpur Malaysia: Oxford Univ. Press

Coughlin, Richard J.
    1960 Double Identity: The Chinese in Modern Thailand Hong Kong: Hong Kong Univ. Press

Cowan, C. D., & O. W. Wolters, editors
    1976 Southeast Asian History and Historiography: Essays Presented to

D.G.E. Hall Cornell, New York: Cornell
Univ. Press

An important collection of studies treating a wide
range of subjects in Southeast Asian studies

Chia, Felix
1980 The Babas Singapore: Times Books
International.

A well written descriptive study of Baba culture
which has an excellent chapter on Baba Malay on
wedding customs, on the game "Cherki" as well as
illustrations of Nonya-ware and Nonya furniture.

1983 Ala Sayang!: A Social History of the Babas
& Nonyas Singapore: Eastern Universities
Press Sdn. Bhd.

Cultural aspects and customs, language and social
patterns of the Baba and Nonyas.

1994 The Babas Revisited Singapore:
Heinemann Asia.

A revised edition of his earlier work The
Babas, focusing mainly upon the Singaporean
Babas.

Chin, John M.
1981a The Sarawak Chinese London: Oxford
Univ. Press.

1988b <u>The Nonya</u> Kuala Lumpur, Malaysia:
Kementerian.

Chew, Daniel
1990 <u>Chinese Pioneers on the Sarawak Frontier:
1841-1941</u> Singapore: Oxford Univ. Press.

Chew, Ernest C. T., and Edwin Lee
1991 <u>A History of Singapore</u> Singapore: Oxford
Univ. Press.

Crissman, Lawrence W.
1967 "The Segmentary Structure of Urban
Overseas Chinese Communities." <u>Man</u>: Vol.
2 (New Series) 185-204.

D.

Dawson, T. R. P.
1969 <u>Tan Siew San: The Man from Malacca</u>
Singapore: Donald Moore Press, Ltd.

de Moubray, G. A. de C.
1931 <u>Matriarchy in the Malay Peninsula and
Neighbouring Countries</u> London:
Routledge & Sons, Ltd.

Ding Choo Ming
1978 "An Introduction to the Indonesian
Peranakan Literature in the Library of the
Universiti Kebangsaan Malaysia" <u>Journal
of the Malayan Branch of the Royal Asiatic
Society</u> Vol. 51.

E.

Edmonds, Juliet
    1968 "Religion, Intermarriage and Assimilation:
        The Chinese in Malaya" Race, Vol. X, I:
        57-67.

    Discusses the role of intermarriage in interethnic
    assimilation among the Peranakan of Malaysia, the
    changing role of Islam in imposing an obstacle on
    this process, and the changing socio-political factors
    in colonial and post-colonial societies that have had
    an effect upon this assimilation.

Edwards, Norman
    1990 The Singapore House and Residential Life:
        1819-1939 Singapore: Oxford University
        Press.

    A very interesting and valuable study of the
    architectural styles and history of Singapore.

Elliott, Allan J. A.
    1955 Chinese Spirit-Medium Cults in Singapore
        Monographs on Social Anthropology, No.
        14, London: The London School of
        Economic and Political Science.

Emerson, Donald K.
    1986 "Southeast Asia": What's in a Name?"
        Journal of Southeast Asian Studies Vol. 19:
        1-21.

Discusses the etymology and political implications of the topographical and areal designation of "Southeast Asia."

Endicott, Kirk Michael
	1970 An Analysis of Malay Magic Oxford: Clarendon Press.

Eng-Lee Seok Chee
	1989 Festive Expression: Nonya Beadwork and Embroidery Singapore: National Museum.

Felix, Alfonso Jr., editor.
	1969 The Chinese in the Philippines, 1570-1770, Vol. I, Manila: Solidaridad Publishing House.

	1969 The Chinese in the Philippines, 1770-1898, Vol. 2, Manila: Solidaridad Publishing House.

Fitzgerald, C. P.
	1965 The Third China Univ. of British Columbia.

Fortier, David H.
	1957 "The Chinese in North Borneo" Colloquium on Overseas Chinese, edited by Morton H. Fried, New York, N.Y.: International Secretariat, Institute of Pacific Relations.

Freedman, Maurice
	1958a Lineage Organization in Southeastern China, Athlone Press.

1959b "The Handling of Money: a Note on the
        Background to the Economic Sophistication
        of Overseas Chinese" <u>Man</u>: 56-7.

1962c "Chinese Kinship and Marriage in
        Singapore" <u>Journal of Southeast Asian
        History</u>, Vol. 3, no. 2.

Deals with the social anthropology of the Babas and
overseas Chinese in Singapore, their kinship
structure, religious practices, language, marriage
practices, and the institution of matrilocality.

1966d <u>Chinese Lineage and Society: Fukien and
        Kwangtung</u> The University of London: The
        Anthlone Press.

Freedman, Maurice & Marjorie Topley
    1961 "Religion and Social Realignment among
        the Chinese in Singapore," <u>Journal of Asian
        Studies</u> Vol. 21: 3-23.

Discusses the history of different Chinese religious
movements in Singapore.

Freedman, Maurice & William E. Willmott
    1961 "South-East Asia: With Special Reference
        to the Chinese," <u>International Social
        Science Journal</u> Vol. 13: 245-270.

Fried, Morton H.

1958 <u>Colloquium on Overseas Chinese</u> New York, N.Y.: International Secretariat, Institute of Pacific Relations.

An early collection of articles about the Overseas Chinese in Borneo, Indonesia, the Caribbean, Peru, Burma, the United States.

Gosling, L. A. P.
1964 "Migration and Assimilation of Rural Chinese" <u>Malayan and Indonesian Studies</u>, edited by John Bastin and R. Roolvink, Oxford: Clarendon Press.

A frequently cited reference that deals with the assimilation and settlement patterns of the rural Peranakan Chinese in the pioneering and subsequent social history of the state of Terengganu in Malaysia.

1983 "Changing Chinese Identities in Southeast Asia" <u>The Chinese in Southeast Asia: Identity, Culture & Politics</u> edited by L. A. Peter Gosling & Linda Y. C. Lim, Singapore: Maruzen Asia, Pte. Ltd.

Gosling, L. A. P. & Linda Y. C. Lim, editors.
1983 <u>The Chinese in Southeast Asia: Ethnicity and Economic Activity</u> Vol. I, Singapore: Maruzen Press, Pte. Ltd.

An important collection of studies about the Overseas Chinese in many different nations of Southeast Asia, focusing upon important theoretical points of their ethnicity, social patterning, and economic orientation.

1983 <u>The Chinese in Southeast Asia: Identity, Culture and Politics</u> Vol. II, Singapore: Maruzen Press, Pte. Ltd.

Gwee, William Thian Hock
1993 <u>Mas Sepuloh: Baba Conversational Gems</u> Singapore: Armour Publishing, Pte. Ltd.

An excellent reference for Baba terms and idiomatic expressions.

H.

Hall, Kenneth & John K Whitmore
1976 <u>Explorations in Early Southeast Asian History: The Origins of Southeast Asian Statecraft</u> Michigan Papers on South and Southeast Asia, No. 11, Univ. of Michigan Press.

Hamilton, Gary
1978 "Pariah Capitalism: A Paradox of Power and Dependence" <u>Ethnic Groups</u>, Vol. 2:1-15.

Treats the political perspective in the creation and exploitation of middlemen minority groups like the Jews of Europe and the Chinese of Southeast Asia.

Harrison, Tom & Stanley J. O'Connor

1970 <u>Gold and Megalithic Activity in Prehistoric and Recent West Borneo</u>, Ithaca, N.Y.: Cornell Univ. Southeast Asia Program.

Ho, Ruth
1975 <u>Rainbow Round My Shoulder</u> Singapore: Eastern Universities Press.

A fast reading narrative of the author's past as a Nonya, with a valuable description of a Peranakan wedding.

Ho, Wing Meng
1976 <u>Straits Chinese Silver</u> Singapore: University Education Press.

An authoritative and exhaustive guide to Straits Chinese silver, showing its range of types and styles, and distinguishing it from Malay silver. Has an interesting description of Baba culture as well. The other books on Straits Chinese porcelain, beadwork and embroidery are colorful, beautiful and interesting guides to Straits Chinese material culture.

The four books below are excellent and colorful authoritative references to Nonya material culture.

1983 <u>Straits Chinese Porcelain: A Collector's Guide</u> Singapore: Times Books International.

1984 <u>Straits Chinese Silver: A Collector's Guide</u> Singapore: Times Books International.

1987 Straits Chinese Beadwork & Embroidery: A
       Collector's Guide Singapore: Times Books
       International.

1994 Straits Chinese Furniture: A Collector's
       Guide Singapore: Times Books
       International.

Holloman, Regina, & Serghei A. Arutiunov, editors.
    1978 Perspectives on Ethnicity Mouton
       Publishers.

Hutterer, Karl L, editor.
    1977 Economic Exchange and Social Interaction
       in Southeast Asia: Center for South and
       Southeast Asian Studies, Michigan Papers
       on South and Southeast Asia, No.13:
       University of Michigan Press.

    An indispensable collection of studies about the
    prehistory and development of traditional Southeast
    Asian civilization as an "interregional system."

Hutton, Wendy
    1995 The Food of Malaysia: Authentic Recipes
       from the Crossroads of Asia Singapore:
       Periplus, Pte, Ltd.

J.

Jiang, Joseph P. L.
    1966 "The Chinese in Thailand" Journal of
       Southeast Asian History Vol. 7, no. 1,
       March.

Johns, A. H.
    1976 "Islam in Southeast Asia: Problems of
        Perspective." <u>Southeast Asian History and
        Historiography: Essays Presented to D. G.
        E. Hall</u> edited by C. D. Cowan and O. W.
        Wolters. Ithaca, N. Y.: Cornell Univ. Press.

K.

Karim, Wazir Jahan
    1990 <u>Emotions of Culture: A Malay Perspective</u>
        Singapore: Oxford Univ. Press.

Kennedy, Jean
    1977 "From Stage to Development in Prehistoric
        Thailand: An Exploration of the Origins of
        Growth, Exchange and Variability in
        Southeast Asia" <u>Economic Exchange and
        Social Interaction in Southeast Asia</u>, edited
        by Karl Hutterer, Michigan: Univ. Michigan
        Press.

Kesseler, Clive S.
    1977 Conflict and Sovereignty in Kelantanese
        Malay Spirit Seances. <u>Case Studies in
        Spirit Possession</u>. Vincent Capanzano and
        Vivian Garrison, editors, 295-332: New
        York: Wiley.

King, Sam
    1992 <u>Tiger Balm King: The Life and Times of Aw
        Boon Haw</u> Singapore: Times Books
        International.

Khoo Kay Kim
    1991 <u>Malay Society: Transformaton &
        Democratization</u> Petaling Jaya, Malaysia:
        Pelanduk Pub. Sdn. Berd.

Khoo Su Nin, editor.
    1989-91 <u>Pulau Pinang: A guide to the local way
        of life & culture of Penang.</u>

    A very rich and informative periodical published in
    Georgetown and devoted largely to the Nonya
    heritage there.

Kobayashi Shinzaku
    1931 <u>Shin Minzoku no Kaigai Hatten Kakyo no
        Kenkyo</u> Tokyo.

Kroeber, A. L.
    1957 <u>Style and Civilization</u> New York: Cornell
        Univ. Press.

Kuchler, Johannes
    1965 "Penang's Chinese Population: A
        Preliminary Account of its Origin and Social
        Geographic Pattern" <u>Asian Studies</u>, Vol. 3,
        no. 3.

L.

Lee, Poh Sing
    1978 <u>Chinese Society in 19th Century Singapore</u>
        Melbourne: Oxford Univ. Press.

Leonard, Jane Kate
>   1984 <u>Wei Yuan and China's Rediscovery of the Maritime World</u> Harvard East Asian Monographs III: Council of East Asian Studies, Harvard Univ.

Lim, Betty
>   1994 <u>A Rose On My Pillow: Recollections of a Nonya</u> Singapore: Armour Publishing Pte. Ltd.

>   Autobiographical account spanning the pre and post war era in Singapore, Malacca and Penang.

Lim, Sonny
>   1982 <u>Baba Malay: The Language of the Straits Born Chinese</u> Master's Thesis, Australia: Monash University.

>   An excellent descriptive analysis of Baba and Pasar Malay.

Lind, Andrew W.
>   1974 <u>Nanyang Perspective: Chinese Students in Multi-Racial Singapore.</u> Honolulu, Hawaii: University Press of Hawaii

M.

Mackie, J. A. C., editor.
>   1976 <u>The Chinese in Indonesia</u> Singapore: Heineman

McCloud, Donald G.
    1986 <u>System and Process in Southeast Asia: The
        Evolution of a Region.</u> Westview Press

McVey, Ruth, editor.
    1963 <u>Indonesia</u> Southeast Asian Studies: Yale
        Univ. Press.

Milner, G B, editor
    1978 <u>Natural Symbols in South East Asia</u>
        London: School of Oriental and African
        Studies.

    An interesting study of the role of symbolisms of
    nature in Southeast Asian culture
Minchin, G.
    1870 <u>Notes and Queries on China and Japan</u>, n.
        s. 4, no. 6 Hong Kong.

Moench, Richard
    1961 "A Preliminary Report on Chinese Social
    and Economic Organization in the Society
    Islands."

    Paper presented at the Tenth Science Congress of
    the Pacific Science Association: University of Hawaii

N.

Nagata, Judith
    1974 "'What is a Malay?' Situational Selection of
        Ethnic Identity in a Plural Society" <u>American
        Ethnologist</u> Vol. 1, no. 2:331-350

1979 <u>Malaysian Mosiac: Perspectives from a Poly-ethnic Society</u> Canada: Univ. of British Columbia Press

Newell, William H
1962 <u>Treacherous River</u> Kuala Lumpur: Univ. of Malaya Press

Ng Siew Hua, Cecilia
1983 "The Sam Poh Neo Neo Keramat: A Study of a Baba Chinese Temple" <u>Contributions to Southeast Asian Ethnography</u>, edited by John R. Clammer, Singapore: National Univ. of Singapore

A valuable ethnographic and ethnological study of a Baba Temple in Singapore, supporting the contention that the Baba's are to be defined as an "ethnic group" rather than as a culture.

O.

Omohundro, John T.
1977 "Trading Patterns of Philippine Chinese: Strategies of Sojourning Middlemen" in <u>Economic Exchange and Social Interaction in Southeast Asia</u>, edited by Karl Hutterer, The Univ. of Michigan Press.

1981 <u>Chinese Merchant Families in Iloilo</u> The Ohio Univ. Press.

Oon, Violet

Peranakan

1978 <u>Peranakan Cooking</u> Singapore: Times
Publications.

P.

Pakir, Anne Geok-In Sim
1987a <u>A Linguistic Investigation of Baba Malay</u>
PhD. Dissertation, Ann Arbor, Mi.:
Dissertation Abstracts International, A: The
Humanities and Social Sciences, 12(1),
June

1988b "The Baba Malay Lexicon: Hokkien
Loanwords in Baba Malay" <u>Applied
Linguistics Association of Australia:
Occasional Papers</u>, 10: 3-30

1989c "Linguistic Alternants and Code Selection
in Baba Malay" <u>World Englishes</u>, Vol. 8,
no. 3, Winter: pages 379-388

1991d "The Range and Depth of English-knowing
Bilinguals in Singapore" <u>World
Englishes</u> Vol. 10, no. 2: 167-179

Png Poh-Seng
1969 "The Straits Chinese in Singapore: A Case
of Local Identity and Socio-Cultural
Accommodation" <u>Journal of Southeast
Asian History</u>, Vol. 10, no. 1.

A much-cited reference that deals with the basic
aspects of Baba Chinese culture in Singapore

Purcell, Victor

>1947 "Chinese Settlement in Malacca" <u>Journal of the Malayan Branch of the Royal Asiatic Society</u> Vol. XX, part 1: 115-125.

>1948 <u>The Chinese in Malaya</u> London: Oxford Univ. Press

An important source talking about Chinese religion in Malaysia, and its history, with an appendix treating Baba Malay.

>1956 <u>The Chinese in Modern Malaya</u> Singapore: Donald More

>1965 <u>The Chinese in Southeast Asia</u> 2nd Edition, London: Oxford Univ. Press

A comprehensive work to be considered a textbook about the Overseas Chinese: their history, demography, social patterning and predicament, in different Southeast Asian countries.

R.

Rabushka, Alvin

>1973 <u>Race and Politics in Urban Malaya</u> Hoover Institution Press.

An important empirical study of urban Malays and Chinese in Kuala Lumpur and Penang, Malaysia, treating their interethnic attitudes and supporting a "transactional hypothesis."

Raybeck, Douglas
     1980 "Ethnicity and Accommodation: Malay-
          Chinese Relations in Kelantan, Malaysia"
          Ethnic Groups Vol. 2: 241-268.

     1983 "Chinese Patterns of Adaptation in
          Southeast Asia" The Chinese in Southeast
          Asia: Identity, Culture & Politics Vol. 2,
          edited by L. A. Peter Gosling & Linda Y. C.
          Lim, Singapore: Maruzen Asia, Pte. Ltd.

Roff, William R, editor.
     1974 Kelantan: Religion, Society and Politics in a
          Malay State Kuala Lumpur: Oxford
          University Press

Roth, H. Ling
     1966 Oriental Silverwork: Malay and Chinese; A
          Handbook for Connoisseurs, Collectors,
          Students and Silversmiths, Kuala Lumpur:
          University of Malaya Press.

     A reprint of an early work done in the twenties that
     shows clear photos of Chinese and Malay silver
     work. An interesting introductory chapter describes
     the traditional techniques and tools of such
     silverwork.

S.

Seah Eu Chin
     1848 "The Chinese in Singapore" Journal of the
          Indian Archipelago

Shellabear, W. G.
1913 "Baba Malay: An Introduction to the Language of the Straits Born Chinese" Journal of the Royal Asiatic Society, Straits Branch no. 65.

Siaw, Lawrence
1981 "The Legacy of Chinese Social Structure" Journal of Southeast Asian Studies, Vol. XII, No. 2, Sept

1983 Chinese Society in Rural Malaysia: A Local History of the Chinese in Titi Jelubu Singapore: Oxford Univ. Press

Simoniya, N. A.
1961 Overseas Chinese in Southeast Asia—A Russian Study Cornell University. An important Marxist study of the political economy of the Nanyang Chinese, their social structure and political history

Siow, Moli
1983 "The Problems of Ethnic Cohesion among the Chinese in Peninsular Malaysia: Intraethnic Divisions and Interethnic Accommodation" The Chinese in Southeast Asia: Identity, Culture & Politics Vol. 2, edited by L. A. Peter Gosling & Linda Y. C. Lim, Singapore: Maruzen Asia, Pte. Ltd.

Skeat, Walter William
    1984 <u>Malay Magic: Being An Introduction to the
        Folklore and Popular Religion of the Malay
        Peninsula</u> Singapore: Oxford Univ. Press.

Skinner, G. William
    1957a "The Chinese of Java" <u>Colloquium on
        Overseas Chinese</u> edited by Morton H.
        Fried, New York, N Y: International
        Secretariat, Institute of Pacific Relations.
        pg. 1-10.

    1963b "The Chinese Minority" <u>Indonesia,</u> edited
        by Ruth McVey. New Haven: HRAF
        Press.

Contains a key theoretical statement about the
"Peranakan social continuum" in Java. Also see
Skinner for comparative work on differential
assimilation between Chinese in Thailand and Java

Somers, Mary F.
    1965 <u>Peranakan Chinese Politics in Indonesia</u>
        Ph. D. Dissertation, Ithaca, N.Y.: Cornell
        University Indonesia Project.

An early work that deals with the formation of a
Peranakan political movement, called "Baperki" in
modern Indonesia.

Somers-Heidhues, Mary F.
    1974 <u>Southeast Asia's Chinese Minorities</u>
        Longman Press.

A valuable overview of the Oversea's Chinese, with discussion of the Baba and Peranakan communities in both Malaysia and Indonesia.

Song Ong Siang
1967 <u>One Hundred Years' History of the Chinese in Singapore</u> Singapore: University of Malaya Press.

Written by a Straits-Chinese, it contains many detailed tidbits about Singapore's past, with reference to the Babas. Contains reprints of early articles by the <u>Straits Chinese Magazine.</u>

Sopie, Mohd. Noordin
1973 "The Penang Secession Movement, 1948-51" <u>Journal of Southeast Asian Studies</u>, Vol. 4.

Southeast Asia Ceramic Society.
1981 <u>Nonya Ware & Kitchen Ch'ing</u> Oxford: Oxford Univ. Press

Steadman, John
1969 <u>The Myth of Asia</u> New York: Simon and Schuster

Steinberg, David Joel
1987 <u>In Search of Southeast Asia</u> Honolulu, Hawaii: Univ. of Hawaii Press

Strauch, Judith
  1980 <u>The Chinese Exodus from Vietnam:
    Implications for the Southeast Asian
    Chinese</u> Boston, Harvard Univ. Press

Judith Strauch has made important theoretical and
empirical contributions to the study of the Overseas
Chinese, to their structural ambiguity and
discrimination by Southeast Asian host societies. All
her work is highly recommended.

  1981 "Multiple Ethnicities in Malaysia: The
    Shifting Relevance of Alternative Chinese
    Categories" <u>Modern Asian Studies</u> Vol. 15,
    no. 2, pp. 235-60

  1981 <u>Chinese Village Politics in the Malaysian
    State</u> Mass.: Harvard Univ. Press.

Suryadinata, Leo
  1981 <u>Peranakan Chinese Politics in Java, 1917-
    1942</u> Singapore: Singapore Univ. Press.

T.

Tan, Chee-Beng
  1979a "Baba Chinese, Non-Baba Chinese and
    Malays: A Note on Ethnic Interaction in
    Malacca" <u>Southeast Asian Journal of
    Social Science</u>, Vol. 7, Nos. 1-2: 19-28.

1980b "Baba Malay Dialect" <u>Journal of the Malayan Branch of the Royal Asiatic Society</u> Vol. 53, Part 1: 150-166.

1982 "Peranakan Chinese in Northeast Kelantan" In <u>The Malayan Branch of the Royal Asiatic Society</u> Vol. 55, part 1.

A study of the rural Chinese in Northeastern Malaysia, comparable with a similar study by Robert Winzeler. A discussion of the building style, the language differences, and the social patterns of the rural Chinese compared to the Malays and the "town Chinese"

1983 "Acculturation and the Chinese in Melaka: The Expression of Baba Identity" <u>The Chinese in Southeast Asia: Identity, Culture & Politics</u>, Vol. 2 edited by L. A. Peter Gosling & Linda Y. C. Lim Singapore: Maruzen Asia Pte. Ltd.

1993 <u>Chinese Peranakan Heritage: In Malaysia and Singapore</u> Kuala Lumpur: Penerbit Fajar Bakti Sdn. Bhd.

A short ethnological style work that highlights the some of the intra-ethnic differences between the Straits settlements, especially of the Babas of Penang

Tan, Giok-Lan
1963 <u>The Chinese of Sukabumi: A Study in Social and Cultural Accommodation</u> Ithaca, New

Peranakan

York: Cornell Univ. Modern Indonesia
Project, Southeast Asia Program,
Department of Asia Studies.

One of the first comprehensive ethnographic studies
of Peranakan Chinese, based in the town of
Sukabumi, on Java. It is a very accurate, detailed
and reliable study, with substantial appendices of
Peranakan kin terms and loan words.

Tan, Rosie Kim Neo
1958 The Straits Chinese in Singapore
Unpublished Dip. Soc. University of
Singapore

An ethnographic study of the Singapore Babas, with
an important definition of baba identity.

Tan, Terry
1981 Terry Tan's Straits Chinese Cookbook
Singapore: Times Books International.

Contains some Nonya favorite recipes and similar
cooking.

Tham Seong Chee
1977 Malays and Modernization Singapore:
Singapore University Press.

Turnbull, C. M.
1972 The Straits Settlements: 1826-67: Indian
Presidency to Crown Colony, University of
London: The Athlone Press.

V.

Vaughn, J. D.
>1854 "Notes on the Chinese of Penang" <u>Journal of the Indian Archipelago.</u>

>1879 <u>Manners and Customs of the Chinese of the Straits Settlements</u> 1971 reprint, London: Oxford Univ. Press.

A widely available, highly readable early account of the Babas and Overseas Chinese in Penang and Singapore. Interesting from the standpoint of colonial attitudes and views of the Chinese, as well as nice descriptions of Chinese secret societies, wedding customs, games, etc.

W.

Wallerstein, Immanuel
>1979 <u>The Capitalist World Economy</u> Cambride: Cambridge University Press

Wallace, Anthony F. C.
>1970 <u>Culture and Personality</u> New York, N. Y.: Random House.

Wang Tai Peng
>1994 <u>The Origins of the Chinese Kongsi</u> Petaling Jaya, Malaysia: Pelanduk Publications Sdn. Bhd.

Wheatley, Paul

1966 The Golden Khersonese: Studies in the
     Historical Geography of the Malay
     Peninsula Before A.D. 1500: Kuala Lumpur,
     Malaysia: University of Malaya Press

An important study of the early documents of the
colonization and exploration of the Malay Peninsula.

Williams, Lea E.
     1964 "Chinese Leadership in Early British
          Singapore" Asian Studies, Vol. 2, no. 2.

     1966 The Future of the Overseas Chinese in
          Southeast Asia New York: McGraw Hill.

Winzler, Robert L.
     1970 Malay Religion, Society and Politics in
          Kelantan PhD. Dissertation, Chicago,
          Illinois.

     1983 "The Ethnic Status of the Rural Chinese of
          the Kelantan" The Chinese in Southeast
          Asia: Identity, Culture & Politics Vol. 2,
          edited by L. A. Peter Gosling & Linda Y. C.
          Lim. Singapore: Maruzen Asia, Pte. Ltd.

     1985 Ethnic Relations in Kelantan: A Study of the
          Chinese and Thai as Minorities Singapore:
          Oxford Univ. Press

Whitmore, J. K.
     1977 "The Opening of Southeast Asia: Trading
          Patterns through the Centuries" Economic
          Exchange and Interaction in Southeast

Asia edited by Karl Hutterer. Michigan: The Univ. Michigan Press

Wickberg, Edgar
1964 "The Chinese Mestizo in Philippine History" Journal of Southeast Asian History Vol. 5, no. 1, March

1965 The Chinese in Philippine Life: 1850-1898 Yale Univ. Press

Willetts, William
1964 "The Maritime Adventures of Grand Eunoch Ho" Journal of Southeast Asian History Vol. 5, no. 2, Sept.

Willetts, William & Lim Suan Poh
1981 Nonya Ware and Kitchen Ch'ing The Southeast Asian Ceramic Society West Malaysia Chapter, Oxford University Press.

Willmott, W. E.
1960 The Chinese of Semarang: A Changing Minority Community in Indonesia Ithaca, N. Y.: Cornell Univ. Press.

1966 "The Chinese of Cambodia" Journal of Southeast Asian History, Vol. 7, no. 1, March.

Willmott, W. E., editor.
1972 Economic Organization in Chinese Society Stanford: Stanford Univ. Press.

Win, Shein
        ?   "The Chinese Community of Burma:
             Problems in Relations between Different
             Ethnic Groups"

Winstedt, Richard
        1961 The Malay Magician: Being Shaman, Saiva
             and Sufi London: Routledge & Paul Kegan

Wolters, O. W.
        1982 History, Culture and Religion in Southeast
             Asian Perspectives ?: Institute of Southeast
             Asian Studies.

        An important theoretical contribution to the history of
        Southeast Asia.

Wood, William, editor.
        1977 Cultural-Ecological Perspectives on
             Southeast Asia Athens, Ohio: Papers in
             International Studies, Southeast Asia
             Series No. 41.

Wu Yuan-li & Wu Chun-hsi
        1980 Economic Development in Southeast Asia:
             The Chinese Dimension, Hoover Institution
             Press

Y.

Yeap Joo Kim
        1993 The Patriarch Singapore: Lee Teng Lay Pte.
             Ltd.

Yeh Hua Fen
    1936 <u>Historical Guide to Malacca</u> Singapore.

A nice discussion of the early Chinese history of Malacca.

Yen Ching-Hwang
    1976 <u>The Overseas Chinese and the 1911 Revolution: With Special Reference to Singapore and Malaya</u> Kuala Lumpur, Malaysia: Oxford Univ. Press

    1981 Ch'ing Changing Images of the Overseas Chinese (1644 -1912) <u>Modern Asian Studies</u> Vol. 15, No. 2:261-285

    1986 <u>A Social History of the Chinese in Singapore and Malaya: 1800-1911</u> London: Oxford Univ. Press

A valuable discussion of Overseas Chinese social structure and its history, treating class, the Kong Si system, religious organization, etc.

Yong, Paul
    1994 <u>A Dream of Freedom: The Early Sarawak Chinese</u> Petalying Jaya: Pelanduk Publications Sdn. Bhd.

Yousof, Ghulam-Sarwar
    1982 "<u>Nora Chatri</u> in Kedah: A Preliminary Report" in <u>Journal of the Malayan Branch of the Royal Asiatic Society,</u> Vol. 55, Part 1:52-61.

INDEX

256

Peranakan

In the world

There are the givers

And then there are the takers

The takers always overtake the givers

But the givers always undertake the overtakers

FINI

Indie Anthropology

Auto-Anthropology
Auto-Anthropology (1992-1998)
A Room In China (2000)
It Makes a Difference (1990)

Anthropological Essays
Anthropological Aesthetics, Rationality,
Ideology & Humanity (1982-1992)
Essays in Anthropological Knowledge (1995)
An Anthropologist in the Larger World (2017)

The Anthropology of Knowledge
Anthropologos & Anthropologia (1992)
Cultural Cybernetics (1996)
Cultural Cognition & Cybernetics (1996)

Archaeological Anthropology
Digging the Past (2002)
Relativity & Relativism (1992)
Southeast Asian Sources (1993)

Ethno-Cultural Studies
Ethno-culture (2005)
Boat People (1986)
The Jetty Chinese (1995)
Malaysian Chinese Ethnoculture (1996)
The Overseas Chinese (2005)
Peranakan (1991)
Nonya (1993)

Symbolic-Linguistic Studies
English & Education (2000)
Language and Culture 1
Language and Culture 2
Language and Culture 3

<u>Lewis Micropublishing Series</u>

1. General System Notebooks

2. Indie Anthropology

3. Robidoux Stories

4. Hugh's Versography

5. Earthbound Primers

6. West Indie Tales

7. Mil-Anth

8. Global Edge

9. Poor Hugh's E-Press

10. Lewis Micropublishing